ABOUT
BOMPAS & PARR

{ Bompas & Parr has embarked on some amazing and fantastical alcohol-inspired projects – from creating dense clouds of breathable cocktail that allow you to become intoxicated through your lungs and eyeballs, to building a church organ that could change the taste of whisky through the power of the music it played, creating a punch for 25,000 people – in a bowl so big that visitors rafted across it before having a glass – and creating a subterranean bar staffed by mermen.

We've built a giant vibrating punchbowl that mixes its contents with the soundwaves that travel through the liquid, conducted experiments where we sent bolts of lightning through cocktails and served whisky on naked bodies (not totally gratuitously – the age of the whiskies was matched to the age of the people).

We've created the world's first collagen-infused gin (along with its signature serve, the Skin 'n' Tonic), brewed a beer flavoured with detritus taken from Roald Dahl's reading chairs, and had to explain ourselves to the authorities after we flavoured a drink with the constituent parts of gunpowder.

We even conceptualized the harp-shaped Guinness beer tap that is now rolling out internationally.

First published in the
United Kingdom in 2019 by
Pavilion
43 Great Ormond Street
London WC1N 3HZ

ISBN 978-1-91162-4844

A CIP catalogue record for this book is available from the British Library

10 9 8 7 6 5 4 3 2 1

Reproduction by ColourDepth Ltd, UK
Printed and bound by Toppan Leefung
Printing Ltd, China

www.pavilionbooks.com

Front cover Peach Gin Fizz page 30
Back cover Champion Cocktail page 108
Page 1 Green Tea & Grain page 48

THE
BOMPAS & PARR
COCKTAIL BOOK

{RECIPES FOR MIXING EXTRAORDINARY DRINKS}

PAVILION

HELLO FROM BOMPAS & PARR 6
OUR TOP TEN DRINKING STORIES 8
BOMPAS & PARR'S TOP TEN GREATEST
MOMENTS IN ALCOHOL 12
TYPES OF COCKTAIL 13
COCKTAIL GARNISHES 18

BAR MENU

{ GIN COCKTAILS 20 }

Sting & Tonic 22
Pink Gin 24
Hanky Panky 24
Gimlet 25
Negroni 26
Mr Twit's Dirty Negroni 28
White Cargo 29
Dry Martini 30
Peach Gin Fizz 30
Orbium Martinez 32
Strawberry & Cream Ramos Gin
Fizz 33
Clover Club 34

{ WHISKY COCKTAILS 36 }

Manhattan 38
Whiskey Sour 39
Mint Julep 39
Old Fashioned 40
Rose Fizz 42
East Meets North 44
Champagne Scotchtail 46
Green Tea & Grain 48
Winter Wonder 50

{ RUM COCKTAILS 52 }

Mojito 54
Dark 'n' Stormy Monk 56
Daiquiri 57
Rum Daisy 57
Nuclear Piña Colada 58

{ VODKA COCKTAILS 60 }

Corrected Espresso Martini 62
Bloody Mary 63
Formula E 64

{ TEQUILA COCKTAILS 66 }

Mezcal Old Fashioned 68
Mexican 55 69
Batanga 70
Paloma 72
Margarita 74

{ **BRANDY COCKTAILS 76** }

Sidecar 78
Sazerac 80
Pisco Sour 82
Shipwreck Sour 84
Iced Tea Club 86
Brandy Crusta 87
Yuzu 75 88
Espresso Cognac-Tail 90
Maple Colada 92
Brandy Snap 94

{ **CHAMPAGNE COCKTAILS 96** }

The Secret of Sabrage 98
French 75 100
Kir Royale 102
Black Velvet Royale 103
Champagne Cocktail 104
Death in the Afternoon 105
Soyer au Champagne 106
Champion Cocktail 108

{ **PUNCHES 110** }

Seafarer's Punch 111
Captain's Punch 112

COCKTAIL BASICS 114
COCKTAIL TECHNIQUES 116
GLASSWARE 121
RESOURCES 125
INDEX 126
FURTHER READING 128
ROLL OF HONOUR 128
PHOTO CREDITS 128

HELLO FROM BOMPAS & PARR

At the beginning of the first edition of this book, published in 2011, we defined alcohol as the universal drug – something that united people and societies across continents and across millennia, providing inspiration and cultural meaning as well as medicinal benefits.

What followed was a riotous, rollercoaster ride around our adventures in alcohol, a no-holds-barred foray into our artistic and commercial collaborations that encompassed everything from ether-based cocktails to a chapter devoted to Buckfast and even a section entitled Getting Drunk on the Cheap.

Some eight years on, the landscape around alcohol has changed somewhat and people, including us, are thinking differently about alcohol. We're collectively drinking less and being more selective about what and when we drink, set against a context of powerful new drivers for healthy living and mental well-being. Young people are increasingly ambivalent about alcohol.

We certainly have no quarrel with those movements, but in spite of this direction of travel it remains clear to us that alcohol retains much of its power as a social lubricant and remains one of the most sophisticated culinary forms. As much as we're respectful of its power to do ill, we continue to unashamedly celebrate alcohol's ability to draw us together. It's not the only thing that can do that, but it remains a darn good one.

So while this book is an evolution of its previous form, and certainly dials back the crazy in some respects, and takes an altogether more grown-up approach to alcohol, it's nonetheless a happy hoorah of its finer points.

The recipes in this book all therefore walk a line that balance our signature, attention-grabbing but considered approach, while offering up some choice twists and predictably unpredictable options. We were also minded to ensure this remained a functional cocktail book, one whose contents remained replicable at home.

We hope you enjoy reading, making and drinking them.

Sam and Harry

OUR TOP TEN DRINKING STORIES

Rather than embark on a comprehensive history of cocktails – far better minds have dived into this more deeply than we ever could – we present some of the top drink-fuelled moments since the dawn of time. We find them pretty inspiring and they have often been used as inspiration for our own style of project and events planning.

1. LORD BYRON'S BOOT (LATE 18TH CENTURY)

Today most people drink from a glass, some from a tankard and, in some bars, from a coconut or a hollowed-out pineapple. Lord Byron drank from a boot. This was no ordinary footwear: Byron's flamboyant eccentricity extended to his taste in drinking vessels, so this boot was black leather with a silver-inscribed rim, a silver spur and heel cap, and a pointed toe for a handle. Byron bought the boot from his mother's side of the family: it was originally given to George Gordon in 1599 and had been passed down the generations.

2. DIANA DEATH JELLY (1997)

One of the most macabre stories to come out of Princess Diana's tragic death was that a funeral technician working on Diana's death mask used it to make a vodka jelly of her face. We have no way to judge on the veracity of this, but, interestingly, moulded and figurative food has played an important role in funerals of the past.

Historically, funeral cakes were made using metal, wood and ceramic moulds with motifs including the three plumes that decorate hearses, roosters (symbolizing resurrection) and Masonic symbols. When we began our professional lives as jellymongers we were particularly interested to hear this story. As we've become more sophisticated in approaching this culinary form, so we've become more respectful of the way jelly can incorporate alcohol and other flavours in a non-liquid form that can convey other storytelling and messaging through its shape.

3. PUSS AND MEW: GIN VENDING MACHINES (EARLY 18TH CENTURY)

As the prices of beer and wine rose in the early 18th century, gin became the drink of choice for Londoners. Parliament passed numerous acts intended to curb the binging and drunken debauchery that followed. But these Gin Acts did little to stop Dudley Bradstreet, who evaded the mandatory Gin Licence by inventing a cunning way to sell gin licence-free on the street. He created what is perhaps the first ever vending machine, marked by the sign of a cat on the wall. Passers-by would put coins in a slot, utter 'Puss! Give me two pennyworth of gin', and hold their cup to the spout until they heard the murmur of 'Mew!' and out came the gin.

4. AMERICAN CONSTITUTION (1787)

Signed on 17 September 1787, the American Constitution is one of the most famous documents ever written. After the final signature was added, the 42 delegates got stuck into their next project: a celebration of epic proportions. Swigging and slurring their way through 54 bottles of Madeira, 60 bottles of claret, 22 bottles of port, 8 bottles of whisky, 8 bottles of hard cider, 12 beers and 7 bowls of alcoholic punch large enough for ducks to swim in, the men earned themselves a place in drinking history.

5. A CIVILIZATION BUILT ON BEER (2580 BC)

Few people realize that the Great Pyramid of Giza, like the other pyramids of Egypt, owes its construction to beer. Labourers in Ancient Egypt were paid a minimum wage, measured in beer. A day's labour was rewarded with two containers of the brew. Some historians say Egyptian beer was brewed from bread (cut up into tiny pieces) and flavoured with dates: a very different taste to that drunk today.

6. WINE BY THE FOUNTAIN (1520)

Not one to do things by half, Henry VIII's court consumed an annual 1240 oxen, 8200 sheep, 2330 deer, 760 calves, 1870 pigs, 53 wild boar and over 2, 700,000 litres/600,000 gallons of beer. In addition to this, Henry VIII drank wine by the fountain – quite literally. At his lavish feasts, wine cascaded down a 4-m/13-ft tall structure for all to drink. In April 2010 historians recreated Henry VIII's octagonal wine fountain in the courtyard of Hampton Court Palace. Based on a well-known painting of the Field of the Cloth of Gold and archaeological excavations, the fountain's exterior is an exact replica but today's fountain uses modern pumps to keep the wine flowing. While the fountain spouts water on weekdays, at the weekend guests can buy a glass of red wine for a small cost. The modern replica is less likely to be surrounded by drunken visitors, but still, as the fountain's motto says: *'faicte bonne chere quy vouldra!'* (let he who wishes make good cheer!).

7. QUAFF FOR YOUR CITY! (1631)

In 1631 the future of a small German city depended on the ability of its citizens to guzzle their drinks. During the Count of Tilly's siege of Rothenburg ob der Tauber, Tilly offered to pardon the city if any of its residents could drink a tankard of wine in one continuous draft. This was no small feat – the tankard he presented held over 3 litres/5¼ pints of wine! Mayor Nusch honoured his people and astonishingly completed the task, saving the city from destruction. Unfortunately the mayor slept in a drunken stupor for the next three days, missing the celebrations, but a well-known Bavarian play, *Der Meistertrunk* (*The Master Draft*), and a daily clock performance in Rothenburg still commemorate his efforts today.

8. PICKLED NELSON (1805)

Vice-Admiral Horatio Nelson won the Battle of Trafalgar but lost his life in the battle: he returned home in triumph but pickled in a barrel of brandy. The ship's supplies provided the best preservative for his body during its journey back to England. After several weeks at sea, the cargo was unloaded and the body was found to be in perfect condition – although legend has it that there was no brandy in the barrel. The crew's liquor rations had been cut back on the journey back to England, but the disgruntled sailors demanded drink: 'your Lordships Petitioners were Served out no provisions or liquor of any kind not even their Allowance of wine!'. The thirsty crew had seemingly drunk every drop from the barrel, giving rise to the phrase 'tapping the Admiral'.

9. THE WORLD'S LARGEST PUNCHBOWL (1694)

Four hogsheads of brandy, 1 pipe of Malaga wine, 20 gallons of lime juice, 2500 lemons, 13 hundredweight of fine white sugar, 5 pounds' weight of grated nutmegs, 300 toasted biscuits, 8 hogsheads of water, 6000 guests and a marble fountain – as commander of the British Mediterranean fleet, based in Alicante, Lord Admiral Edward Russell concocted the world's largest punch (and it was to be more than 300 years before his record was broken – by Bompas & Parr in London in 2010). Unable to find a punchbowl large enough, Russell sought inspiration in his garden and settled on a fountain to serve his colossal brandy punch at an officers' party. Small boys served drinks from wooden canoes, paddling through the punch for only 15 minutes at a time lest they were overcome by the fumes. Guests took a week to drink the fountain dry. The only pause in the celebrations was when it started to rain and a silk canopy was erected to stop the punch from being watered down.

10. THE BEER FLOOD OF 1814

On 17 October 1814 the streets of London were flooded with dark ale. Meux's Horse Shoe Brewery of Tottenham Court Road once stood on the site of what is now the Dominion Theatre. A gigantic vat 6.7 m/ 22 ft tall and 18 m/60 ft in diameter and big enough to hold 4000 barrels of beer was built to trump rival brewers. The ale had been maturing for many months when one of the 29 supporting hoops snapped, followed by another, then another, releasing a tidal wave of over 600,000 litres/132,000 gallons of beer. Buildings crumbled and innocent people were swept away: the death toll at the scene reached nine. Rescue attempts were further thwarted as thousands of thirsty Londoners packed the streets. Riots broke out in hospitals, where other patients caught the scent of beer-soaked casualties and demanded their fair share. Then when the dead bodies were exhibited to a paying public, so many people crowded into the room that the floor collapsed and the death toll was pushed higher. A judge ruled the event an 'Act of God', making this beer flood an official natural disaster.

BOMPAS & PARR'S
TOP TEN GREATEST MOMENTS
IN ALCOHOL

1. Architectural Punchbowl, for Courvoisier: we flooded a Regency townhouse with nine tons of punch, so big you could row a boat across its surface.

2. Alcoholic Architecture: our own bar featuring a walk-in cocktail cloud, featuring inhalable gin and tonic.

3. The Flavour Conductor, for Johnnie Walker: a pipe organ, inspired by Aldous Huxley's *Brave New World*, that can change your sense of taste as you drink whisky.

4. 10,000-year-old ice, for Johnnie Walker: harvesting glacial ice to serve with Johnnie Walker Blue Label.

5. Anatomical Whisky, for the Ace Hotel: naked people masqueraded as drinking vessels, with whisky the same age as them licked off by complete strangers as they recounted their life stories.

6. Cocktail Monolith: a vending machine that dispensed cocktails designed to match with your personality, based on a psychology-based interface.

7. Mr Twit's Odious Ale: brewing a beer flavoured with the detritus found down the back of Roald Dahl's writing chair.

8. Anti-A'Gin, for Warner Leisure: the world's first gin flavoured with collagen, alongside its signature serve, the Skin 'n' Tonic.

9. Chladni Punchbowl: an 80-litre/140-pint punchbowl that vibrates to the tune of deep bass notes to mix its own contents while exhibiting beautiful standing wave patterns on the surface of the liquid.

10. The Big Harp, for Guinness: conceptualizing the new Guinness beer dispense fount – the thing that the beer is dispensed from. Our 'big harp' is now rolling out around the world.

TYPES OF COCKTAIL

This book doesn't attempt to be an exhaustive range of cocktails, but offers a selection that is close to our hearts, partly as they are either classics which you should know how to make, or they have been given our own twist for a special event, dinner, party or commercial collaboration.

To demystify cocktails and help you make your own drinks from whatever there is to hand, we have divided the cocktail repertoire into a number of types. These are Sours, Martinis, Old Fashioneds, Punches, Highballs, Champagne Cocktails and Flips/Blended/Warm. Master the idea behind each style of drink and it's easy to busk around the theme, substituting alternative spirits and mixers.

SOURS

Common sours include the Whiskey Sour (bourbon, lemon, sugar) and the Daiquiri (rum, lime, sugar). You can make variations on sours by replacing the sugar syrup with grenadine syrup or a liqueur like Cointreau or maraschino. The Sidecar (cognac, lemon juice, Cointreau) uses Cointreau to sweeten and balance the cognac and lemon juice as well as introducing orange flavours to the mix. If you use grenadine to sweeten a sour it gives you a Daisy; if you use pineapple juice you'll have made a Fix.

Sugar syrup can be replaced with other types of sweeteners: honey, agave syrup or even jam. When using a thicker sweetener you need to be careful that you get all the ingredients fully mixed before adding any ice, as the ice can prevent sugars mixing with other ingredients. If you think about the way honey behaves at different temperatures (runny when hot, stiff when cold) you'll get the idea.

There are plenty of other cocktails that are based on sours. Fizzes (like the Ramos Gin Fizz) are effervescent sours shaken for an arm-achingly long time, served in a highball glass and topped up with soda water. Collins are stirred directly in a large highball, iced and topped up with soda water. When you lengthen a sour, turning it into a Fizz or a Collins, you may need to add more sugar and citrus, otherwise the cocktail will be lacking in flavour.

MARTINIS

Martini-style cocktails, if classically made, are undoubtedly potent but filled with subtle flavours.

Martinis are classically made with gin, vermouth and bitters. Mixing a spirit such as gin with a little vermouth totally transforms the spirit by softening the alcohol and opening up the flavours.

Most of the time they are stirred with ice, sometimes shaken, and in both cases benefiting from a degree of dilution as they gain chill. A direct Martini is the punchiest of all as it involves no contact with ice (and therefore no dilution) at all – this involves simply freezing the spirit, pouring it into a glass and adding a spritz of vermouth and a couple of drops of bitters.

Simple Martini-style cocktails include the classic Dry Martini (gin or vodka, dry vermouth and bitters), the Manhattan (whiskey, sweet vermouth, bitters) and their relations (the Martinez or Aviation in the Dry Martini's case, the Rob Roy in the latter). Drinks like the Negroni (gin, sweet vermouth, Campari) also fit into this category: feel free to apply the term to cocktails made with other liquor bases too.

Various other drinks are often called Martinis, such as fruit-driven drinks like the Watermelon Martini or French Martini, but these are not strictly speaking Martinis at all and won't be as potent, even if they are tasty.

A Martini can be adjusted in sweetness by using either Italian (sweet) vermouth, French (dry) vermouth, or a mixture of both for a 'perfect' cocktail. It's worth trying different types of vermouth, as the range of flavours is immense, and use quality brands like Dolin, Noilly Prat or Belsazar. Vermouths oxidize fairly quickly, so keep yours in the fridge, and once opened, discard the bottle after a few weeks. The same goes for sherry!

However, when people ask for a Dry Martini they are really commenting on how little vermouth they want in their cocktail, not what type it is. Serious advocates of the Dry Martini include Sir Winston Churchill (whose recipe was allegedly to fill a martini glass with iced gin – an example of a Direct Martini – and simply glance at a bottle of vermouth) and Kingsley Amis (who suggested 15 parts gin to 1 part vermouth).

In practice, the ratio of spirit to vermouth can be anywhere from 2:1 gin to vermouth to perhaps as much as 5:1, but any more than that and you are showing off.

OLD FASHIONEDS

Old Fashioneds work on the principal of adding a little bit of sugar or sugar syrup and a few dashes of bitters to spirits. To this extent they completely manifest the definition of a cocktail as a mixture of spirits, sugar, water and bitters. The drink is built (assembled in its final glass) by stirring it with ice cubes, progressively adding more cubes as the first ones are diluted, over some minutes. This simple act performs something of a miracle, mellowing out all but the roughest spirits.

While the Old Fashioned itself is a American whiskey-based cocktail, using an Orange or Angostura bitters-soaked sugar cube, it is a great example of where the technique works brilliantly well with all other types of spirit, from rum to vodka or tequila.

The appeal of a drink where you don't need any special equipment needn't be spelled out. These drinks are also readily pre-batchable, so they're perfect for parties, if potent. If batching, ignore ice for now, and simply extrapolate the ingredients to the quantities you want, stir them together, add an additional 10% total volume in water for dilution, then chill it all. To serve, simply pour over fresh ice and add a garnish.

PUNCHES

Punches are easy to make. Simply follow this sea shanty-type rhyme.

One of sour   *A dash of bitters*
Two of sweet   *A sprinkle of spice*
Three of strong   *Serve well chilled*
And four of weak   *with plenty of ice*

As the rhyme suggests, this category of drinks is pretty versatile but should result in a balanced drink, whatever quantity you make it in. You can slam in anything to hand that fulfils the various criteria and it should work out just fine.

Sour should be obvious – think citrus juice. Sweet should be equally obvious – think sugar syrup, honey, agave, liqueurs or jams. Strong is obviously whatever spirit you are using. Even with the weak component, you have plenty of options – this could be water, soda, tea, fruit juice or champagne. As for bitters, Angostura bitters is classically Caribbean, so that fits, but these days there are so many good quality bitters (such as The Bitter Truth and independent brands such as Bob's Bitters) that you can't go far wrong. For spice, a grating of fresh nutmeg always works, and so does allspice, mace or cinnamon.

Pour the pre-mixed punch over a single large block of ice in a large vessel. It is a crowd-pleaser and will act as a memorable centrepiece.

HIGHBALLS
Arguably the simplest of mixed drinks, these are built in the glass and require no special skills at all. Think G&T, whisky and soda, or rum and Coke. These are not cocktails in the traditional sense of the word but, like many mixed drinks, have come to be known under this catch-all, too. You can, judiciously, add further flavours, and not just through garnishing, and credibly still call it a highball. A bar spoon of syrup, for example, could lift your drink to the next level.

CHAMPAGNE COCKTAILS
As the name suggests, Champagne cocktails tend to combine some or all the classic components of a cocktail (spirit, sweetener, citrus and bitters) but bring it to life with the effervescence of bubbly. They are invariably built (mixed in the glass in which it is to be served) in flutes.

FLIPS/BLENDED/WARM
This final category is something of a catch-all for us, to showcase three styles of drinks that don't neatly fit into the other groupings. Flips traditionally contain a whole egg but, as we show, you can create a creamy mouthfeel without adding a raw egg; blended drinks are mixed in electric blenders, commonly associated with tropical (tiki) drinks; and warm cocktails channel a wintry seasonal vibe.

SOUR
spirit + citrus juice + sugar

MARTINI
spirit + vermouth + bitters

OLD FASHIONED
spirit + sugar + bitters

PUNCH
spirit + sweet + sour + weak

HIGHBALL
spirit + mixer

CHAMPAGNE COCKTAIL
spirit + sweet + champagne

COCKTAIL GARNISHES

Garnishes are an integral part of the drink, the finishing touch that adds visual appeal, character and potential talkability. The idea is that the garnish is a further amplification of the taste profile of a drink, and that it is edible. Beyond that, the world is your oyster and you can use whatever you want to finish the drink. Less is, normally, more, although sometimes it is still acceptable to use a tiki cocktail umbrella.

'...AND AN ORANGE TWIST'

One of the most commonly called for and easy-to-process is citrus zest or peel – lemon, lime, orange or grapefruit. If a drink calls for a citrus zest garnish, the idea is to cut thin strips of peel, carefully avoiding the bitter pith, and squeeze them over the drink to release their aromatic oils, also rubbing the zest around the rim and/or stem of the glass. You can then either discard the zest or drop it into the cocktail. Only use fresh and unwaxed fruit.

GARNISHES 101

WHEEL OR SLICE – a round cross-section of the fruit

HALF WHEEL – as above, cut in half

QUARTER WHEEL – as above, cut into quarters

WEDGE – a chunk of fruit, cut lengthways, placed on the rim of the glass

TWIST OF ORANGE OR LEMON ZEST – as described above

SPRIG OF MINT – make sure all the leaves are fresh

CHERRY – Luxardo makes a fine liqueur-soaked cherry, a long way from some of the sticky neon-coloured horrors which are more widely available

---

SWEET

Adding sweetness to drinks makes them more palatable, works in tandem with sour flavours (see below) to add complexity, and amplifies all flavours. Sweetness comes in many forms, including fruit juices, but often recipes will simply call for sugar syrup, AKA simple syrup. You can buy this at most supermarkets, and certainly online, in various quantities, but it's also super easy to make yourself.

TO MAKE YOUR OWN SUGAR SYRUP

On a hob, combine equal weights of sugar and water, bring to the boil, ensuring all crystals are dissolved, then cool and bottle. It should keep for a week in a sterilized bottle when stored in the fridge.

SOUR

The corollary of sweet is sour. Most of the time, we are talking citrus, and that means lemon or lime juice. If you're making a large number of cocktails, it's far more efficient to hand squeeze a job lot into a small jug and reserve it to one side than squeeze to order. It needn't be said that fresh juices are essential to good cocktails and that shop-bought pasteurized variations, or pre-packaged 'sour mixes', are not OK.

Remember that the strength of lemon and lime juice can vary radically depending on the individual fruit. As you get more accomplished you might choose to adjust your recipes accordingly.

GIN
COCKTAILS

The simplest way to think of gin is as neutral alcohol (like vodka) that has been flavoured with herbs and spices. What was once known as Mother's Ruin, and then became a drink for your grandmother, gin has now regained its stature as an essential part of the cocktail repertoire and is a perfect place from which to start exploring cocktails. Gin is a versatile spirit and lends a satisfyingly clean flavour to a cocktail.

The gin distillation process is fairly straightforward: a neutral grain spirit is redistilled with an increasingly wide array of botanicals such as (classically) orange zest or peel, orris root, cardamom, coriander seed, cinnamon, cassia bark, liquorice and others, all centred around juniper, which must remain the hero of the mix.

Sometimes the botanicals are left to infuse in the spirit before distillation, and sometimes the botanicals don't go into the still but are placed in a basket above the still and the vapours passed through them. Sometimes further infusions are added post-distillation. Every brand will tell you their method is the best.

It's worth experimenting with different gins to find the taste profile that works for your palate, and that works with the drink. Some gins are perfect for Martinis (Plymouth, say), others 'disappear' when you add tonic (we find Bombay Sapphire makes a great G&T).

There is such a range of tonics available these days. Suffice to say we aren't alone in loving Fever-Tree, preferring the 'full fat' version over the light – there's ultimately no wrong answer and the answer is what you like, so all we do is encourage you to experiment with the increasingly large ranges and styles on sale.

STING & TONIC

Here's our creative twist on a classic cocktail, using a historic English culinary staple – and traditional outdoor foe. Stinging nettles are notorious for their stinging power, but they have been used to make beer and wine for centuries.

They seem to grow anywhere, and for most of the year (though during autumn and winter they can be quite bitter so it's best to make a syrup or cordial from the newest tips in early summer, but don't pick them if they're flowering). By late summer they will be coarse and bitter.

Armed with some thick gloves, fill a bucket's worth of nettle tips and add them to a large saucepan with 1.5 litres/2¾ pints of water, a cup of Earl Grey tea, grated ginger, lemon zest and a stick of liquorice root. Add 1.5 kg/3 lb 5 oz of golden caster sugar, and when it's fully dissolved, cool, strain and bottle the mix. If your bottle is sterilized the nettle cordial should keep for a year.

Then when it's time for a G&T, upgrade to the Sting & Tonic.

50 ml/2 fl oz Bombay Sapphire gin
15 ml/½ fl oz nettle cordial
Top with tonic
Fresh nettle tips to garnish

Build in a copa glass, pouring the gin over cubed ice, then adding the cordial and finally the tonic. Garnish with fresh nettle tips, and a thistle if you can find one. Serving with a sustainable straw protects the lips from being stung.

For a regular G&T, fill a highball with ice, squeeze over a wedge of lime before dropping it in the glass, pour on 50 ml/2 fl oz gin and then top with tonic.

PINK GIN

Originally a pink gin was not iced but was balanced with equal parts water to dry gin. The pink colour comes from Angostura bitters. Modern palates prefer the chill of ice. Vary the amount of bitters to taste from 3 dashes to 8 or more. As ever, adding a bar spoon of sugar syrup helps the medicine go down, but it's not essential.

50 ml/2 fl oz gin
6 dashes Angostura bitters
1 bar spoon of sugar syrup (optional)
Twist of lemon zest to garnish

Stir the gin, bitters and sugar syrup (if you choose) with ice cubes in a mixing glass, then strain into a chilled martini or cocktail glass. Garnish with a twist of lemon zest.

HANKY PANKY

This Martini variation is a beast of a cocktail to knock back in the morning. It was created by the Savoy Hotel's first head bartender, Ada Coleman, who reigned at the American Bar from its opening in 1898. Impressively, there have been only 11 head bartenders in the entire history of the American Bar. This is a great reviver.

40 ml/1½ fl oz gin
20 ml/⅔ fl oz sweet vermouth
2 dashes Fernet Branca
Large twist of orange zest to garnish

Stir the ingredients in a mixing glass over cubed ice and strain into a martini glass. Garnish with a large twist of orange zest.

GIMLET

{ The lime cordial in a Gimlet (pronounce it
Gim with a hard 'g' rather than 'gym') acts to
simultaneously sweeten and sour the gin. If you
want to get fancy you can make your own cordial
using fresh lime juice and sugar syrup; however, we
like Rose's cordial as the brand has an inspirational
history, and we're in good company as the best
bartenders in history also called for it. The Rose
family were Scottish shipbuilders. In 1867, after a
bout of naval deaths from scurvy, the Merchant
Shipping Act made it compulsory for all ocean-
going ships to provide rations of lime juice. The
Roses, seeing a sailing-related opportunity, set
up a subsidiary selling preserved lime juice. To
meet demand for their cordial they bought a lime
plantation in Dominica – and used their ships to
transport the lime juice back to Britain.

50 ml/2 fl oz gin
30 ml/1 fl oz Rose's Lime Cordial
10 ml/2 tsp lime juice
Wheel of lime to garnish

Shake the ingredients well with cubed ice. Either
strain into a martini glass or serve with cubes of ice in
an old-fashioned glass. Float a lime wheel on the surface
of the drink.

NEGRONI

The Negroni was invented by Count Camillo Negroni, a gambler, wastrel and cowboy who returned to his native Italy from America once Prohibition was enforced. He liked to have his Americano cocktail served with gin rather than with soda, hence his version came to be called by the name Negroni.

The thing that is really intriguing about the Negroni is the colour derived from Campari: a glorious and startling red. This colouring, at least originally, comes from E120, otherwise known as carmine or cochineal, made by crushing thousands of tiny cochineal insects and extracting the colour. Food manufacturers like it as it is powerful, readily soluble in water, organic and doesn't fade, though Campari stopped using cochineal more than a decade ago.

45 ml/1½ fl oz gin
45 ml/1½ fl oz sweet vermouth
45 ml/1½ fl oz Campari
Twist of orange zest to garnish

Pour all the ingredients into an old-fashioned glass over ice cubes. Stir well and garnish with a twist of orange zest.

MR TWIT'S DIRTY NEGRONI

{ This drink comes from an immersive theatrical performance and dinner that we collaborated on, to mark what would have been the centenary of Roald Dahl's birth. As one of our favourite authors, and the source of a whole host of food-based inspiration (from Willy Wonka to James and the Giant Peach), we were delighted to bring some of his most disgusting characters to life. This was the partner to the equally dubiously named Mrs Twit's Special Milk. In this case, the earthy notes of mezcal justify the 'dirty' nomenclature.

This one works best by pre-batching.

200 ml/7 fl oz Campari
200 ml/7 fl oz sweet vermouth
200 ml/7 fl oz mezcal (Del Maguey is a good
  one)
Twist of orange zest to garnish

Add the ingredients, along with 100 ml/ 3½ fl oz mineral water, to a 700 ml/1¼ pint glass bottle. Refrigerate.

To serve, measure out 60 ml/2½ fl oz and pour it over cubed ice into an old-fashioned glass. Express the oils from a piece of orange zest over the drink and then drop it in the glass.

WHITE CARGO

One of our favourite ice cream cocktails is the White Cargo. It's a really straightforward recipe and everyone loves it when you put ice cream in cocktails – as a culinary technique it was initiated by the famed Victorian French chef Alexis Soyer (see page 106) so it has some credibility beyond novelty's sake. Gin and ice cream is delicious, no two ways about it. This cocktail is great for pre-batching.

Serves 20
2 litres/3½ pints vanilla ice cream
1 750-ml/26-fl oz bottle gin
180 ml/6 fl oz maraschino liqueur
Freshly grated nutmeg to garnish

Put all the ingredients into a punch bowl. Wait until the ice cream has mostly melted, stir and then top with grated nutmeg. Ladle it into teacups.

This can also be made in smaller quantities: use the same ratios but either shake the ingredients together (without ice) or use a blender as if making a milkshake.

DRY MARTINI ➦

{ Some would say this is the ultimate cocktail. It's certainly an acquired taste as it packs a meaty punch. We've seen drinkers familiar with fruity 'Martinis' floored when they encounter a true Martini. After all, it's mostly spirit. Experiment with the ratio between spirit and vermouth to find your perfect pairing (see page 14).

60 ml/2½ fl oz gin
15 ml/½ fl oz dry vermouth
Twist of lemon zest to garnish

Add gin and vermouth to a mixing glass, cover with ice and stir well – for about 30 seconds. Strain into a martini glass and garnish with a twist of lemon zest.

PEACH GIN FIZZ   *(see cover image)*

{ A super-fruity cocktail with a silky mouthfeel.

50 ml/2 fl oz gin
30 ml/1 fl oz lemon juice
20 ml/⅔ fl oz peach nectar
1 medium egg white (20 ml/⅔ fl oz egg white)
20 ml/⅔ fl oz soda water

Shake the first four ingredients for 10–15 seconds to emulsify the egg white. Then add a handful of ice to the shaker, and shake again for 10–15 seconds. Fine strain into an old-fashioned glass over cubed ice. Finally, add a splash of soda to give an extra frothy top to the drink.

ORBIUM MARTINEZ

The Martinez is the elder sibling to the Martini, and arguably more palatable and flavourful than its precursor. We created this variation on the recipe for the launch of Hendrick's Orbium gin – a gin containing quinine, wormwood and blue lotus blossom – a botanical we'd previously used in the Plant Connoisseurs' Club at Kew Gardens, and said to increase your visual perception of colour.

40 ml/1½ fl oz Hendrick's Orbium gin
15 ml/½ fl oz Barolo Chinato aperitif wine
10 ml/2 tsp sweet vermouth
5 ml/1 tsp Maraschino Liqueur
1 dash Angostura bitters
Twist of orange zest to garnish

Add all the ingredients to a mixing glass, add a scoop of cubed ice and stir for 25 seconds. Strain into a chilled Nick 'n' Nora glass and garnish with an orange twist.

STRAWBERRY & CREAM RAMOS GIN FIZZ

{ Created for an Instagram-targeted event for Häagen-Dazs, this twist on the classic Ramos Gin Fizz is a guilty secret of ours.

50 ml/2 fl oz Strawberry gin
12.5 ml/2 tsp lemon juice
12.5 ml/2 tsp lime juice
30 ml/1 fl oz Strawberry Cheesecake ice cream
20 ml/⅔ fl oz egg white
2 drops orange blossom water
2 drops rose water
Top with soda water
Rose petal and slice of strawberry to garnish

Add all the ingredients apart from the soda to a cocktail shaker. Dry shake the mix first (shake without ice), then add a good scoop of cubed ice and shake again. Shake for ages – enough for your arms to get tired – this drink needs it! Strain into a mini coupe and then top with soda – this creates a vividly creamy head. Garnish with a rose petal and a slice of strawberry.

CLOVER CLUB

A crowd-pleaser from the late 19th century and which boasts a bar named in its honour in Brooklyn, New York. The egg white gives it a layer of unctuous foam when you shake it. When adding egg white to a cocktail it's recommended to shake it without ice first – known as a dry shake – to get everything thoroughly mixed, and then shake again with ice. The raspberries break up in the shaker and give the drink a nice pink hue.

50 ml/2 fl oz gin
4–5 raspberries
15 ml/½ fl oz sugar syrup (see page 19)
15 ml/½ fl oz lemon juice
1 egg white
1 raspberry to garnish

Dry shake all the ingredients, then shake again with cubed ice and double strain into a coupe glass. Garnish with a final raspberry placed in the foam.

{ WHISKY COCKTAILS }

Whisky or whiskey (spelled without an 'e' for Scotch, Japanese and English and with one for American, Irish or Canadian) used to be seen as last-drink-of-the-night territory, drunk neat, by men around a fire. How times change! Today, all types of whisky can be drunk neat or in mixed drinks (and, of course, by both sexes). It's not a new concept but it has taken a while to bed in – it used to be that American whiskies were more commonly used in mixed drinks. This is partly because in the golden ages when cocktails were being developed, old world whiskies from Scotland and Ireland wouldn't have been so readily available to mixed drinks pioneers.

Scottish whisky (Scotch) and Irish whiskey are traditionally based on barley, although many include other grains, such as wheat.

Rye whiskey is the original spirit for cocktailing and is made mainly from rye grains (of course). It's slightly harsh on the palate but this is an advantage in mixed drinks as it makes its character felt. Although rye went out of fashion for making cocktails during Prohibition in the 1920s, it's now making a comeback and is the connoisseur's choice for a good Manhattan cocktail.

Bourbon is made from corn (maize) and is normally much sweeter than rye. When making a cocktail with bourbon, less sugar is needed: the bourbon will carry the day.

MANHATTAN

{ The Manhattan is a whiskey-based
Martini. You can serve it either in a
martini glass or with cubes of ice in an
old-fashioned glass. The usual sweet, dry
or 'perfect' vermouth business applies
(see page 14). Traditionalists always use
rye to make a Manhattan. Being British,
we like making Rob Roys – replacing the
whiskey with Scotch and garnishing with
a cherry.

60 ml/2½ fl oz rye or bourbon whiskey
15ml/½ fl oz sweet vermouth
2 dashes Angostura bitters
Cherry and a twist of lemon zest to garnish

Stir the ingredients with ice cubes in a
mixing glass. Strain into a chilled cocktail
glass. Garnish with a cherry and a twist of
lemon zest.

WHISKEY SOUR

{ You need to shake a whiskey sour hard to get a decent foam on it: 30 seconds is about right. You can also add in some egg white and dry shake it first. The egg white adds a creamy consistency and a fine white foam top layer.

60 ml/2½ fl oz bourbon whiskey
15ml/½ fl oz lemon juice
15ml/½ fl oz sugar syrup (see page 19)
1 egg white (optional)

Add all the ingredients to a shaker. Shake hard, and then strain into an ice-filled old-fashioned glass.

MINT JULEP

{ Traditionally this was served in a pewter or silver julep cup. It's a great, cooling drink as it's made over crushed ice, but it's a strong one as there are no other liquid components except for melting ice water. If you've got lots of mint in the garden, you can feel smug that you've practically home-grown this cocktail.

2 sprigs of mint
15ml/½ fl oz sugar syrup (see page 19)
75 ml/2½ fl oz bourbon whiskey

In either a highball glass or a silver julep cup, gently press the leaves of one sprig of mint with the non-spoon end of a bar spoon into the sugar syrup, making sure you coat the insides of the glass.

Fill the glass with crushed ice, add the bourbon and churn it all up with a bar spoon. Top with additional crushed ice, then garnish with the second sprig of mint.

OLD FASHIONED

{ The Old Fashioned is the original way of making rough booze
more palatable by adding sugar and bitters. The traditional
method is to wet a sugar cube with bitters and a little water and
stir until it dissolves. This can be a bit of a bore – sugar syrup is
much easier and gives a better result. Be warned, this recipe is
pretty punchy!

45 ml/1½ fl oz bourbon whiskey
30 ml/1 fl oz rye whiskey
10 ml/2 tsp sugar syrup (see page 19)
3 dashes Angostura bitters
Twist of orange zest to garnish

Pour the bourbon into a heavy-bottomed old-fashioned glass with
two or three ice cubes and stir for 10 seconds. Now add the other
ingredients, and a couple more ice cubes, and keep stirring. Add a final
ice cube, then express the oils from a piece of orange zest over the
drink and then drop it in the glass

ROSE FIZZ

{ This was developed by us as part of a signature
range for David Beckham's Haig Club whisky –
a grain (wheat-based) Scotch whisky rather than
the traditional barley. The range is designed to
make whisky approachable and easy to drink. This
drink, and Green Tea & Grain on page 48, are both
delicious and totally unlike any other whisky cocktail
you may have tried.

1 white sugar cube
2 drops rose water
30 ml/1 fl oz Haig Club Single Grain Scotch whisky
60 ml/2½ fl oz brut champagne

Build in a champagne flute as if for a classic champagne
cocktail. First drop in the sugar cube, then soak it with
2 drops of rose water. Next add the whisky, then top
with champagne.

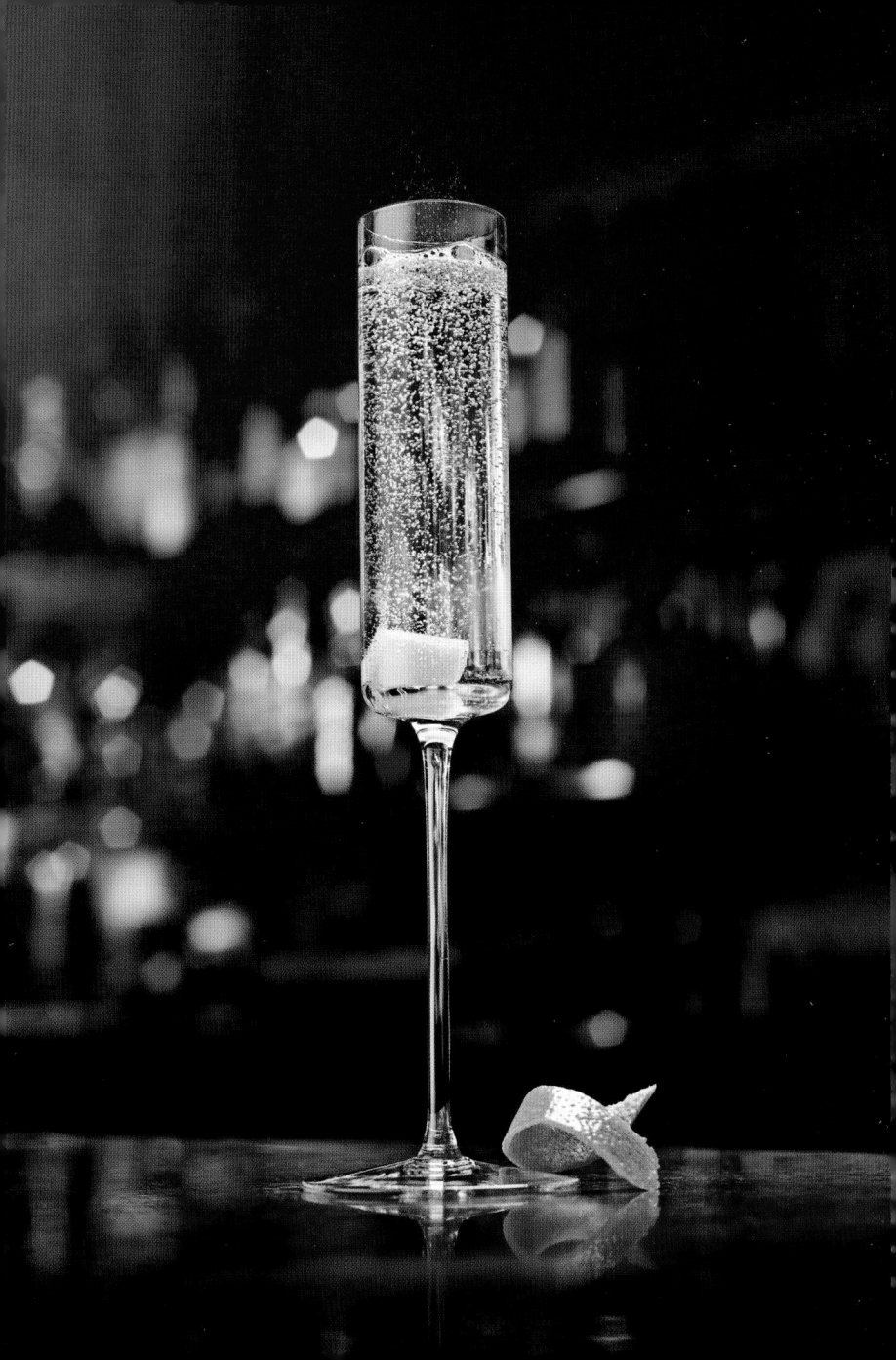

EAST MEETS NORTH

{ This is a whisky punch that follows the classic punch rhyme:
'one of sour, two of sweet, three of strong, four of weak'.
Parts, that is. Super easy to remember and you can't go wrong
with it even when you aren't using rum, the spirit it was
originally intended for.

To follow the rhyme, assemble the following ingredients in
a shaker:

One of sour: 15 ml/½ fl oz lemon juice
Two of sweet: 30 ml/1 fl oz sugar syrup (see page 19)
Three of strong: 45 ml/1½ fl oz Johnnie Walker Black Label blended
   Scotch whisky
Four of weak: 60 ml/2½ fl oz jasmine tea
Jasmine or other edible flower to garnish

Shake the ingredients with a handful of ice cubes and serve in a
cocktail glass or pour over fresh ice cubes in a highball. Garnish with
a flower, ideally a jasmine flower.

CHAMPAGNE SCOTCHTAIL

{ A classic champagne cocktail traditionally pairs brandy and champagne. It's not rocket science to switch out the brandy for whisky – grasp that methodology and you are well on the way to becoming a master mixologist yourself. Indeed, as you become more accustomed to making cocktails you'll start noticing the similarities between many cocktails.

This one has added appeal as it contains edible gold dust, and the effervescence of the champagne provides a perpetually self-churning effect that looks particularly alluring.

Sugar cube rolled in gold shimmer dust
40 ml/1½ fl oz blended Scotch whisky
150 ml/5 fl oz non-vintage brut champagne

Place the sugar cube at the bottom of a champagne flute, then pour over the whisky, followed by the champagne.

GREEN TEA & GRAIN

{ Green tea is a delicate accompaniment which works well with lighter styles of whisky. This highball is super refreshing. A variation on this drink is to pair whisky with coconut water as an alternative to green tea.

50 ml/2 fl oz Haig Club Single Grain Scotch whisky
2 dashes orange blossom water
20 ml/⅔ fl oz cold-brewed green tea
Sliver of fresh ginger or a twist of orange zest to garnish

Build in a highball glass over cubed ice. Pour over the whisky first, then add the orange blossom water and then the green tea. Garnish with a sliver of fresh ginger or an orange twist.

WINTER WONDER

{ A creamy mouthfeel and a warming wintry flavour profile: it's the best egg nog you've ever tasted, without an egg, which we have found to be rather polarizing among drinkers!

40 ml / 1½ fl oz Baileys Original
30 ml / 1 fl oz Jameson Whiskey
10 ml / 2 tsp port (or Carpano Antica Formula sweet vermouth)
10 ml / 2 tsp maple syrup
30 ml / 1 fl oz double cream
Freshly grated nutmeg and 1 cinnamon stick to garnish

Shake all the ingredients in a shaker with a scoop of ice cubes. Strain into an old-fashioned glass and garnish with a dusting of freshly grated nutmeg and a cinnamon stick, if you like.

{ RUM COCKTAILS }

Rum is distilled from sugar cane juice and molasses, the treacly waste product of crystal sugar manufacture. Dark rich rums are aged in wooden barrels; golden rums undergo less aging; clear, light rums may be unaged (these are rather fierce) or aged to smooth out the flavours, then filtered to remove the colour and hangover-inducing impurities.

Former French colony Martinique produces a rum called *rhum agricole*. As this is made from raw sugar cane juice and no molasses (like the Brazilian version *cachaça*) it is lighter and more vegetal, and from experience can deliver bewilderingly savage hangovers.

Don't be afraid to go tropical on the ingredients you put with your rum. It's invariably from an island paradise so it's OK to splash in coconut juice, spicy ginger brews, puréed mango – and garnish with a leafy pineapple top. This is the essence of tiki. We love tiki. It is bawdy and brilliant. All those Samoan war clubs, bamboo and broken bits of boat strapped to the ceiling.

Many rum cocktail recipes call for a raft of different rums: white, golden and aged rums from exotic places like Jamaica, Cuba and Barbados. Don't be daunted. Mixing together a few different styles of rum can make for a far more complex drink, but if you don't have a drinks cabinet heaving with rare and unusual distillates, crack ahead with what you've got.

MOJITO

{ This is one cocktail where it's better to use sugar rather than sugar syrup – the sugar crystals lacerate the mint as you muddle and it releases a lot of flavour. It's a refreshing drink – a light sour that has been lengthened with lots of soda. It's traditional to make it in the glass that you are serving it in. It originates from Cuba and was a favourite drink of the writer Ernest Hemingway when he lived there in the 1940s.

Large sprig of mint
60 ml/2½ fl oz white rum
30 ml/1 fl oz lime juice
2 tsp white caster sugar
Top with soda water
Wedge of lime and fresh mint leaves to garnish

Put 5–6 mint leaves in the bottom of a highball glass, and use the non-spoon end of a bar spoon to gently bruise (but not crush) the leaves. Pour over the rum, lime juice and sugar. Next, fill the glass with crushed ice and churn the mix with your spoon. Top with soda, add extra crushed ice to ensure a good pile is showing above the rim of the glass, then finally garnish with a wedge of lime and tuck the remainder of your mint leaves in among the ice.

DARK 'N' STORMY MONK

{ This twist on a Dark 'n' Stormy is another
cocktail recipe from Alcoholic Architecture's
ecclesiastically-styled and monastic cocktail
collection.

50 ml/2 fl oz Old Monk Rum
15 ml/½ fl oz St Elizabeth Allspice Dram Liqueur
Top with ginger beer
Wedge of lime to garnish

Build the cocktail in an old-fashioned glass, pouring the
rum over ice cubes, then the allspice liqueur and finally
top with ginger beer. Garnish with a wedge of lime.

DAIQUIRI

{ A Daiquiri is a rum sour made with lime juice. Harry makes this with Havana Club 7-year Old Rum, mainly because he brought some back after a trip to Cuba and has never switched. It's not a light rum (which is traditionally used in Daiquiris) but it makes a tasty drink.

60 ml/2½ fl oz Havana Club 7-year Old Rum
10 ml/ 2 tsp sugar syrup (see page 19)
10 ml/2 tsp lime juice

Shake the ingredients with ice cubes and strain into a chilled martini or cocktail glass.

RUM DAISY

{ Daisies first gained popularity in the late 19th century, initially as a brandy and citrus pairing, but as you can see it's a highly adaptable format. This one is summer in a glass and certainly a crowd pleaser.

40 ml/1½ fl oz white rum
10 ml/2 tsp triple sec
20 ml/⅔ fl oz lemon juice
20 ml/⅔ fl oz sugar syrup (see page 19)
2 fresh raspberries
Twist of lemon zest to garnish

Add all the ingredients to a shaker, add a handful of cubed ice, and shake for 15 seconds. The vigour of your shake will break up the raspberries. Strain it into a coupette and garnish with a twist of lemon zest.

NUCLEAR PIÑA COLADA

{ This cocktail is at its best when served in a hollowed-out pineapple. Use small pineapples that you have hollowed out and frozen first. You can use the juice in the cocktail – but you'll need a juicer, as without one pineapples are a bore to juice. A blender is the usual way of making a piña colada but if you don't have one just shake with crushed ice. If you happen to have more ingredients to hand then ring the changes with a mixture of light and dark rums, or a dash of double cream. This nuclear version uses the punchy flavours of an overproof (high strength) rum (more than 60% abv), so you don't need much at all.

20 ml/⅔ fl oz Wray & Nephew Overproof Rum
30 ml/1 fl oz Boiron Pineapple Purée
20 ml/⅔ fl oz Green Chartreuse
10 ml/2 tsp Velvet Falernum
80 ml/3 fl oz coconut water
20 ml/⅔ fl oz lime juice
20 ml/⅔ fl oz sweetened coconut cream (Coco Lopez)
Pinch sea salt
Wedge of pineapple, maraschino cherry and a cocktail umbrella to garnish

Pour all the ingredients into a blender and blend for 15–20 seconds, then pour into a hollowed-out pineapple. Garnish with a pineapple wedge, maraschino cherry and a cocktail umbrella.

{ VODKA COCKTAILS }

More than any other spirit, vodka has attracted consumers' admiration and ire in equal measure. Having arguably helped drive the recent cocktail revolution, with myriad brands appearing, each boasting a purer taste profile than the next, and in turn driving the trend toward premiumization, vodka has more latterly suffered in the craft stakes and for precisely its lack of flavour. It's what turned people to gin and made it the predominant craze of the last decade.

Suffice to say that not all vodkas taste the same, and that it remains an essential pre-requisite to your drinks cupboard. To the former, if you were to line up a variety of good-quality vodkas, you would immediately be able to discern differences in flavour, mouthfeel and source organic material, be it potato (Chase), wheat (Absolut), barley (Sipsmith) or other (could be rice, rye, sorghum or other grains). To the latter, once you mix vodka with other ingredients, you may no longer be able to discern this nuance, but it is a wonderful vehicle for those other pairings, amplifying and extending taste and flavour and adding that alcoholic hit along the way.

Flavoured vodkas, once big business, are now seen as slightly naff – unless they manage to convey their craft credentials. Be sure to use naturally flavoured variants.

CORRECTED
ESPRESSO MARTINI

{ This was inspired by the modern classic cocktail, the Espresso Martini, invented in the 1990s by renowned bartender Dick Bradsell for a supermodel who had requested a drink that would 'wake her up and fuck her up'.

Make sure you use freshly made espresso. See also Espresso Cognac-Tail on page 90 for another twist on the Espresso Martini.

30 ml/1 fl oz vodka
30 ml/1 fl oz Kahlua
20 ml/⅔ fl oz sugar syrup (see page 19)
50 ml/2 fl oz espresso

Shake and strain the ingredients into a Duralex tumbler. Serve with a shot glass of 'correction fluid' (grappa mixed with cream and white chocolate liqueur, made to a 1:1:1 ratio, looks like correction fluid, hence the name) on the side and sip the two drinks alternately.

BLOODY MARY

{ American cocktail king Dale DeGroff recommends 'rolling' tomato-based drinks rather than shaking or stirring. Rolling means pouring the drink back and forth between two vessels. The idea is to stop foam forming and the juice separating.

The origins of the Bloody Mary are hotly disputed among those in the know, who variously argue that it was either invented in Paris in the 1920s, or popularized in New York by the same bartender in the following decade. Either way, they concede that vodka and tomato juice may have been a pre-existing cocktail, even if the spices came later.

If you don't have vodka, replace it with gin. If you plump for gin it's called a Red Snapper.

60 ml/2½ fl oz vodka
120 ml/4 fl oz tomato juice
Squeeze of lemon juice
Freshly ground salt and black pepper to taste
Tabasco sauce to taste
Worcestershire sauce to taste
Celery stick to garnish

Put all the ingredients into a mixing glass with ice cubes and pour or 'roll' into another mixing glass, holding the ice within the first mixing glass using a julep strainer; now pour it back into the first glass containing ice and repeat several times. Strain into a large ice-filled highball glass. Garnish with a celery stick and a fresh, coarse grind of black pepper.

FORMULA E

{ This was created for the organisers of Formula E to mark the race's return to London in 2016. We served it along the top corridor of Tower Bridge to the epic backdrop of our home city.

This is an excellent example of how vodka acts as a flavour vehicle. For the original drink we included a touch of the eco-friendly saline algae Formula E uses to power its electricity generators to lend the drink its blue-green hue. You can simply add a little blue foodcolouring to convey the colour of electricity.

The 'electrified' vodka is simply Absolut Citron lemon-flavoured vodka infused with Japanese Sancho pepper. Pour 25 or so of these peppercorns into a bottle of the stuff and leave for a couple of days to add some zingy spice. If you can get some Szechuan buttons, even better – these taste like you're licking an 8V battery, a comparison which you'll either 'get' or will not.

60 ml/2½ fl oz 'electrified' Absolut Citron vodka
15 ml/½ fl oz triple sec
30 ml/1 fl oz lemon juice
1 medium egg white (20 ml/⅔ fl oz egg white)
2–3 drops blue food colouring

Dry shake all the ingredients to emulsify the egg white, then add ice cubes and shake again. Fine strain into a chilled coupe glass. For Formula E we garnished the drink with some blue-coloured Sancho pepper-flavoured popping candy.

{ TEQUILA COCKTAILS }

Tequila might still suffer from an evil reputation, but it's ill-deserved and outdated. Over the last decade it's been moving from a drink you'd expect to shoot, to one you'd expect to savour in cocktails, or to sip neat. No longer do we associate tequila with bottles of cheap spirit that have a worm inside (to prove it was at least alcoholic enough to preserve the creature, even if that didn't assure on taste and flavour). So give it another go, otherwise you are missing out on a strange and wonderful distillate that makes elegant cocktails.

Tequila is made from a desert plant commonly called a cactus. It is not a cactus, just very like one. Agave is, in fact, related to the lily. Tequila comes in different styles depending on how it has been made and how it has been aged. Really you should only drink tequilas that are made with blue agave (*Agave tequilana*). The label on the bottle will proudly state the fact if that is the case! (See also A Word on Mezcal overleaf.)

The youngest and lightest tequila is Blanco (white), which is bottled immediately after distillation, and Plata (silver), which is bottled within two months of distillation; Reposado (rested) tequila is aged between two months and a year in oak barrels; a mixture of Blanco or Plata and Reposado is called Joven (young) or Oro (gold); a more expensive category is Añejo (aged), which is aged between one and three years in small oak barrels. There is also a new super-premium category called Extra Añejo (extra aged), which is aged for a minimum of three years in oak barrels.

Añejo and Reposado grades are excellent for cocktails where you want to showcase the spirit. Get the balance right and Blanco can be awesome, too.

MEZCAL OLD FASHIONED

{ You can make an Old Fashioned cocktail with any spirit, and using tequila in this way helps you get to know the spirit in an appropriately mellow way. You can also experiment with reducing the amount of tequila and replacing it with mezcal.

60 ml/2½ fl oz Reposado tequila (or 45 ml/1½ fl oz Reposado tequila and 15 ml/½ fl oz mezcal)
1 bar spoon agave nectar
1 dash Angostura bitters
Twist of orange zest to garnish

Pour half the tequila into a heavy-bottomed old-fashioned glass with two or three ice cubes and stir for 10 seconds. Now add the other ingredients, and a couple more ice cubes, and keep stirring. Add a final ice cube, then garnish with a twist of orange zest.

A WORD ON MEZCAL

Mezcal is tequila's rustic cousin. While tequila is technically a mezcal, which claims the name for the entire category of spirits made from agave plants, it is merely one type of mezcal made to specific rules, mainly in the Jalisco region of Mexico, using the blue agave (*Agave tequilana*) only. Look for '100% blue agave' on the label, otherwise it may be a 'mixto' and contain other sugars (and may be more likely to give you a hangover).

Mezcal as a product also refers to the smokey spirits that are made from 50 or so other varietals of agave, such as tobala, sotol, espadin, arroqueño and barril. In total there are more than 250 species of agave, but only 50 are used in alcohol. Production methods that include open-air fermentation, earthen ovens, open flame-fired clay stills and so on contribute to mezcal's intense character, which is an acquired but popular taste.

MEXICAN 55

{ The Mexican equivalent of the French 75 (see page 100), this recipe similarly involves mixing spirit, sugar, citrus and champagne. It's totally delicious.

Lime juice and caster sugar for the glass rim
30 ml/1 fl oz Blanco tequila
12.5 ml/2 tsp maraschino liqueur
12.5 ml/2 tsp lime juice
Top with brut champagne

Use a champagne flute. As with a French 75 (see page 100), you can moisten the outside of the glass rim with lime juice and roll it in caster sugar.

To make the cocktail, pour the first three ingredients into the glass, give a quick stir, and then top with champagne.

Variations on this recipe open up a world of additional flavours. Serve it on the rocks with a few slices of cucumber; make it in a flute and add a couple of bar spoons of beetroot juice, one of our favourite and most unexpected combinations; or you can add a bar spoon of a herbaceous liqueur such as Chartreuse, or a rooty one like Aperol.

BATANGA

{ Tequila, Coca-Cola and lime juice: the tequila equivalent of a Cuba Libre. A pinch of salt adds to mouthfeel and makes it rehydrating in hot climates. We particularly like this version as it's traditionally stirred with a bloody big chef's knife at La Capilla bar in Tequila town in Mexico.

50 ml/2 fl oz tequila (your choice whether
  Blanco or Reposado)
Top with Coca-Cola
Squeeze of ½ a lime
Pinch of salt
Wedge of lime to garnish

Build this cocktail over cubed ice in a highball glass. You don't have to use a knife to stir it but we like the drama. Garnish with a wedge of lime.

PALOMA

{ This is essentially a Margarita that has been lengthened with fruit juice and soda. If ever you need to convert a naysayer to tequila, this is the sort of drink that could change his or her mind – sweet but peppery and piquant.

50 ml/2 fl oz Blanco tequila
10 ml/2 tsp agave syrup
10 ml/2 tsp lime juice
30 ml/1 fl oz pink grapefruit juice
Top with soda water (grapefruit soda if possible)
Twist of grapefruit zest to garnish

Shake the first four ingredients with ice cubes and strain over cubed ice in a highball glass. Top with soda water or pink grapefruit soda if possible. Garnish with a twist of grapefruit zest.

MARGARITA

{ Delicious and adaptable, the Margarita is the workhorse of tequila. It is arguably the most popular cocktail in the USA, though they don't really drink tequila like this in Mexico – they just sip it straight. Many theories surround its origin – from being named for a Texan socialite in 1948 to being created in Tijuana for a star of the silent screen called Marjorie King, Margarita being the Spanish for Marjorie. Others suggest it emanated from 1930s Hollywood, or may simply be a Spanish translation of the 'daisy' category of drinks, Margarita being also Spanish for daisy.

A slice of lime and sea salt for the glass rim
60 ml/2½ fl oz Blanco tequila
30 ml/1 fl oz Cointreau
30 ml/1 fl oz lime juice

Start by rubbing a slice of lime around half of the outside rim of your glass and then carefully roll the same part of the rim through a plate of coarse sea salt. To make the cocktail, shake the ingredients with ice cubes and strain into the glass. Alternatively, make it in exactly the same way but serve it on the rocks in an old-fashioned glass.

To enhance this basic recipe, you can choose any number of variations. You can vary the liqueur used or add in other sweeteners, from agave syrup (making it a Tommy's Margarita) to a spoonful of jam; alter the types of citrus used; add in some easily breakable fruit into the shaker like raspberries, strawberries, some chunks of watermelon, fig or try a purée instead; add some heat with chilli; or top with champagne. Don't be afraid to be adventurous.

{ BRANDY COCKTAILS }

Since the dawn of time alchemists have probed the mysteries of the occult to find the secret of eternal life. While they failed to discover the philosopher's stone, they managed to transform base wines into fiery spirits using the technique of distillation. These spirits miraculously preserved the heart of fragile fruits and offered those who drank them the chance of transcendental escape – and the one spirit that epitomises this approach best is cognac.

Brandy can be distilled from any fermented fruit juice, so it's hardly surprising that there is a huge range in terms of flavour and quality as you range from French to Spanish. Germany has schnapps made from various fruits and eastern Europe has slivovic made from plums.

However, most cocktails that include brandy are looking for grape- or apple-based distillates. Cognac is distilled from wine made in the Cognac region of South-West France. It comes in various grades look for the letters near the brand name. VS (Very Special) is aged in wood for at least two years and is best for cooking; VSOP (Very Superior Old Pale) is aged in wood for at least four years and is a good choice for making cocktails; then there is XO (Extra Old) for sipping and, if you're feeling decadent, mixing.

France also produces armagnac, which uses wine from the Gascony region; it is similarly graded but a little more savage than cognac owing to arguably more rudimentary production techniques.

Cognac was used in many early cocktails and mixed drinks and has a long history as a party pleaser. Sadly, it fell into neglect when the phylloxera aphid hammered French wine production in the late 19th century and the world turned its attention to whisky.

SIDECAR

{ The sidecar is really just a Brandy Sour in which
the sugar syrup is replaced by orange liqueur.
We've suggested a ratio that we like, but you could
go for equal parts (the most usual way) or hit the
cognac hard, depending on your mood (or whether
it's decent brandy). It's worth sugaring the rim of the
glass first, as the added sweetness really helps the
flavours come together.

Lemon juice and caster sugar for the glass rim
50 ml/2 fl oz Rémy Martin VSOP cognac
30 ml/1 fl oz orange liqueur (Cointreau or Grand Marnier)
30 ml/1 fl oz lemon juice
5 ml/1 tsp sugar syrup (see page 19)
Twist of orange zest to garnish

First, moisten the outside rim of a martini or cocktail
glass with lemon juice, then roll it in caster sugar. Shake
all the ingredients with ice cubes. Strain into the glass and
garnish with orange zest.

SAZERAC

{ The Sazerac, an old-fashioned style of cocktail, has
  always been New Orleans' cocktail of choice. It
was originally made with the French cognac Sazerac
de Forge et Fils, but cognac became hard to obtain
after the phylloxera aphid struck French vineyards in
the 1880s and American rye whiskey took its place.
If you want to create a traditional American Sazerac,
you should use Sazerac Rye Whiskey, Peychaud's
Bitters (invented in New Orleans) and Herbsaint
pastis instead of absinthe.

1 splash absinthe
45 ml/1½ fl oz Rémy Martin cognac (XO or at least VSOP)
1 tsp sugar syrup (see page 19)
3 dashes Angostura bitters

Splash the absinthe into an old-fashioned glass, swirl it
and then pour it away. This will give a good hit of absinthe
on the nose, but it won't overpower the rest of the drink.
Place the glass in the freezer to chill down. Combine the
remaining ingredients in a mixing glass filled with ice
cubes and stir well. Strain into the absinthe-coated glass.
No garnish is required.

PISCO SOUR

{ The Pisco Sour is an excellent egg-based cocktail made with pisco, a clear grape-based brandy made in Chile and Peru.

60 ml/2½ fl oz pisco
30 ml/1 fl oz lime juice
30 ml/1 fl oz sugar syrup (see page 19)
1 egg white
2 dashes bitters to garnish

Put all the ingredients, except the bitters, into a shaker. Remove the spring from a Hawthorne strainer (see page 119) and shake all the ingredients, together with the spring, but without ice. The spring helps to create a firm foam. Remove the spring, top the shaker up with ice cubes, shake again, then strain into a martini or coupe glass. Dot the bitters on to the foam.

SHIPWRECK SOUR

{ This was created for Beyond the Waterfall, our underwater-themed bar staffed by mermen. It features a British cider brandy aged in casks recovered from a shipwreck off the coast of South Africa in 2007.

10 ml/2 tsp Somerset Shipwreck Cider Brandy
50 ml/2 fl oz Calvados
20 ml/⅔ fl oz Crème de Pêche
20 ml/⅔ fl oz lemon juice
20 ml/⅔ fl oz egg white
Edible flowers to garnish

Assemble all the ingredients in a shaker, dry shake (without ice), then shake again with ice cubes and strain into a coupe glass. Garnish with an edible flower or two.

ICED TEA CLUB

{ Make this summery drink with shop-bought iced tea – your guests will never know.

45 ml/1½ fl oz Rémy Martin VSOP cognac
7.5 ml/1½ tsp Cointreau
Top with peach or mango iced tea
Fresh peach slices to garnish

Build this cocktail in a highball and garnish with fresh peach.

BRANDY CRUSTA

{ This is a 19th-century cocktail which has stood the test of time and still works for modern palates. It also boasts a rather wonderful presentational technique which is not shared by any other drink – whereby you insert half a hollowed-out lemon into your glass so that it almost becomes an extension of the glass.

Lemon juice and caster sugar for the glass rim
½ a lemon, hollowed out for the glass
60 ml/2½ fl oz VSOP cognac
15 ml/½ fl oz orange curaçao
15 ml/½ fl oz lemon juice
15 ml/½ fl oz maraschino liqueur
2 dashes Angostura bitters

First, prepare a wine glass by moistening the outside rim with lemon juice and rolling the rim in caster sugar. Then insert the lemon half inside the glass so that it sticks up above the rim. Shake the ingredients with ice cubes, then strain into the glass. Sip through the lemon, and if it's too sour you can lick off some of the sugary rim, too.

YUZU 75

{ We were asked by Rémy Martin to reinvent cognac in cocktails. While cognac is one of the oldest cocktail components, it has progressively fallen out of favour and has come to be known as a neat sipping spirit. We think that's all wrong and really enjoyed the task of making it appealing once again through some light and refreshing drinks.

40 ml/1½ fl oz Rémy Martin VSOP cognac
10 ml/2 tsp yuzu juice
15 ml/½ fl oz sugar syrup (see page 19)
Top with brut champagne, or sparkling sake
Edible flowers to garnish

Shake the first three ingredients with ice cubes, then strain into a stemless flute glass and top with champagne. Garnish with an edible flower or two.

ESPRESSO COGNAC-TAIL

{ The Espresso Martini is conventionally a vodka-based drink. We thought we could get a deeper layer of flavour by using cognac.

50 ml/2 fl oz Rémy Martin VSOP cognac
10 ml/2 tsp dark crème de cacao
30 ml/1 fl oz espresso
5 ml/1 tsp brandied cherry juice (or Luxardo maraschino cherry juice)
2 dashes Sour Cherry bitters
Fresh mint leaf to garnish

Shake all the ingredients with ice cubes and strain into a martini glass. Garnish by floating a single mint leaf on the top of the drink.

MAPLE COLADA

{ This is your choice as to whether you make this cocktail shaken with ice for a cool, creamy drink, or literally blended to make something of a dessert-style cocktail.

50 ml/2 fl oz Rémy Martin 1738 cognac
5 ml/1 tsp maple syrup
10–15 ml/2–3 tsp sweetened coconut cream (Coco Lopez)
Freshly grated nutmeg to garnish

Shake all the ingredients with ice cubes and strain into a wine glass – or blend the ingredients with 4 cubes of ice only. In both cases, garnish with freshly grated nutmeg.

BRANDY SNAP

{ This is a good cocktail for a cold winter's day, or for those who aren't fans of mulled wine at Christmas. Go carefully with the butter, which adds a creamy mouthfeel: remember you can always add more, but you can't take it away.

40 ml/1½ fl oz Rémy Martin VSOP cognac
40 ml/1½ fl oz boiling water
20 ml/⅔ fl oz Drambuie
5 dashes Angostura bitters
Small knob of butter
10 ml/2 tsp double cream
Brown sugar to taste
Freshly grated nutmeg to garnish

Blend and heat all the ingredients in a Nespresso-style Aeroccino machine or simply combine all the ingredients in a glass coffee cup, stirring until the butter has dissolved. Garnish with freshly grated nutmeg.

{ CHAMPAGNE COCKTAILS }

*'It is always safest to ask your guests what they would like to drink.
If they say that they do not mind it means they want Champagne.'*
Harry Craddock, *The Savoy Cocktail Book*, 1930

The beauty of champagne arguably lies more in the expense,
celebratory opening ritual and the fact that the carbonated beverages
get your guests intoxicated quicker, than its very taste. A team from
the University of Surrey gave subjects equal amounts of sparkling
and flat champagne containing the same levels of alcohol. Five
minutes after downing the drink, the group who'd had sparkling
champagne had 54 milligrams of alcohol in their blood, while those
on the flat stuff had only 39 milligrams. The bubbles carry alcohol
into the lungs so it can go straight into the bloodstream, bypassing
the liver. Party on!

Champagne and champagne cocktails are generally acceptable with
almost any foods and at any time of the day. They are also simple to
make. For the purposes of champagne cocktails, use non-vintage
brut champagne. Sweeter alternatives are best for sipping and
appreciating, a taste profile most of us are no longer quite used to
(champagne used to be made far, far sweeter than it is today).

THE SECRET OF SABRAGE

{ For extra style points when opening a bottle of champagne, try sabrage. This involves knocking the top of the champagne bottle off with the blade of a sabre.

It's important to note that it's not simply brute force that's at work here, but physics: the contact of sabre to glass at the right point concentrates the force at the weakest part of the bottle – where the neck joins the body of the bottle. Once you initiate a crack, the pressure within will force the top off.

Done correctly, it will sheer clean off. If you're left with shards of spikey glass, it's possible that fragments will have entered the liquid and you should probably discard it. Fail!

Here are some key steps to master:

1. Remove the foil from the bottle, making sure there's no sticky residue left along the seam of the bottle at this point.
2. Invert the bottle and place it neck down in a bucket of crushed ice. Leave for one hour.
3. When you're ready to perform, loosen the cage covering the cork from the bottle, move it up over the glass ridge and do it up tight again above this ridge.
4. Hold the bottle in your non-dominant hand horizontally with the seam facing upwards.
5. Holding the sabre, chef's knife, belt buckle or other metal device (it really doesn't matter as long as it's got some weight and weft behind it, and has a hard edge that can connect with the glass ridge). This is the weak spot where there's a 'stress concentration' point.

6. Practise sliding your blade along the seam, tracing it from the base of the bottle to that lip. Make sure that you retain contact between sabre and glass. This ensures that vibrations in the glass are concentrated at that weak spot.

7. When you've practised the sabre's journey a few times, you are ready. But when you actually go for it, you'll want to follow through with your sabre arm. Hopefully you'll hear a pop and the cork and cage will fly out some 5–10 metres/15–30 feet, propelled by the 90 pounds per square inch of pressure inside the bottle and the 250 million bubbles of carbon dioxide that are craving to be released. Using this method a skilled swordsman will lose little champagne.

CHAMPAGNE BOTTLE SIZES

Magnum	2 bottles – 1.5 litres
Jeroboam	4 bottles – 3 litres
Rehoboam	6 bottles – 4.5 litres
Methuselah	8 bottles – 6 litres
Salmanazar	12 bottles – 9 litres
Balthazar	16 bottles – 12 litres
Nebuchadnezzar	20 bottles – 15 litres

FRENCH 75

{ This is a gin sour lengthened with champagne.
Traditionally it was made with cognac but it's more
popularly made with gin.

40 ml/1½ fl oz gin
20 ml/⅔ fl oz lemon juice
20 ml/⅔ fl oz sugar syrup (see page 19)
Top with brut champagne
Strip of lemon zest to garnish (optional)

Shake the first three ingredients with ice cubes and strain
into a champagne flute, before topping with champagne.
You could consider garnishing with an extra long peel of
lemon zest, known as a horse's neck.

KIR ROYALE

{ The secret here is to ensure you use proper crème de cassis which comes from Burgundy. This has a depth of character and dry notes amid the sweetness, which pairs well with champagne.

2 bar spoons crème de cassis
Top with brut champagne
Twist of lemon zest to garnish

Pour the cassis into a champagne flute and top with champagne. Garnish with a twist of lemon zest.

BLACK VELVET ROYALE

{ The original Black Velvet cocktail was developed for a
gathering at Brooks's Club, London, in December 1861. Prince
Albert, Queen Victoria's husband and the Prince Consort,
had just died and the barman insisted that the drinks should
be black to match members' mourning clothes. Black Velveet
was conceived as a drink with a 50:50 ratio of champagne
and Guinness, but we've always thought that a polarizing
combination. Working on a project for Guinness, we came across
a 'taste bridge' that marries the two liquids together.

This recipe can work with whatever berry liqueur you have to
hand – crème de cassis is great, but crème de mûre (blackberry),
framboise (strawberry), Chambord (raspberry) and others
would work just as well, with a matching berry on the side of
the glass to garnish.

5 ml/1 tsp crème de cassis or equivalent
80 ml/3 fl oz Guinness
80 ml/3 fl oz brut champagne

Build the three components in the order listed above in a champagne
flute. You may need to flow the beer and the champagne down the
stalk of a bar spoon – this should prevent either liquid from bubbling
over in the glass.

CHAMPAGNE
COCKTAIL

{ A true elegant classic, which combines some of the finer things in life and signals that you are just as sophisticated. If you're ever in a bar and have no idea what to drink or are flummoxed by a cocktail menu, this is always a good shout as all good bartenders should have what it takes to make to hand and know how to make it.

1 sugar cube
2 dashes Angostura bitters
30 ml/1 fl oz VSOP cognac
Top with brut champagne
Twist of orange or lemon zest to garnish

Place the sugar cube in a champagne flute, soak it with bitters, then add the cognac and top up with champagne. Garnish with a twist of orange or lemon zest.

DEATH IN THE AFTERNOON

{ Invented by Ernest Hemingway while
stuck out in a rough sea one day, Papa's
suggestion was to 'drink three to five of
these slowly'. You can add a dash of sugar
syrup (see page 19) if you think it needs
a bit of extra sweetness.

15 ml/½ fl oz absinthe
Top with brut champagne

Pour the absinthe into a champagne flute and
top with champagne.

SOYER AU CHAMPAGNE

{ One of our culinary heroes is the Frenchman Alexis Soyer, very much the celebrity chef of the Victorian era. He revolutionized the modern kitchen (championing gas cookery) while working at the Reform Club in London, he invented a mobile soup kitchen to feed victims of the Irish Potato Famine and saved troops from malnutrition in the Crimean War, working alongside Florence Nightingale. He also wrote best-selling books, manipulated the media and launched products such as Soyer's Nectar, a blue lemonade sold as a health drink.

Soyer was a flamboyant self-publicist who adopted the zig-zag as his signature glyph. All his clothes were cut on the bias, dishes were topped with zig-zag attelets (small, ornamental skewers) and even his pastries bore the pattern.

His greatest adventure came during London's Great Exhibition of 1851. Soyer, the leading celebrity chef of his day, was offered exclusive rights to the catering for the Crystal Palace built in Hyde Park. He refused, because influence from the temperance movement meant that alcohol was not allowed to be served with meals. Soyer didn't think you could have a civilized meal without booze. So he chose instead to create his own Great Exhibition of food at Gore House, adjacent to Hyde Park. He ambitiously called it Soyer's Universal Symposium of all Nations and it was effectively a food and drink theme park. It included an ice cave with stalactites of real ice that had to be shipped in daily (at the time there was no refrigeration) and stuffed snow foxes, a medieval banqueting hall, a weather chamber where arcs of electricity fizzed across the ceiling imitating sheet lightning, and a grotto you had to plunge through a waterfall to reach. Entrance to the grotto was free but you'd get wet unless you hired one of Soyer's umbrellas.

The Symposium, though spectacular, was hugely overambitious and ended amid massive financial complications. It did, however, bring mixed drinks and cocktails to the attention of London society. One of the few lucrative elements was the Washington Bar attached to the Symposium. The blades of society could choose from over 40 beverages, which included some of Soyer's own inventions, one of which was the Soyer au Champagne.

1 tbsp vanilla ice cream
10 ml/2 tsp maraschino liqueur (we use Luxardo)
10 ml/2 tsp orange curaçao
10 ml/2 tsp brandy
Top with brut champagne
Slice of orange and a maraschino cherry to garnish

Build the first four ingredients in a champagne flute and then top with champagne. Garnish with a slice of orange and a cherry. Think of it as a champagne float. Decadent? *Mais, oui.*

CHAMPION COCKTAIL

{ Here's a variation we created for G. H. Mumm and Formula E, leveraging the classic winner's podium wreaths – hence the name – made traditionally with bay leaves.

1 bay leaf
20 ml/⅔ fl oz sugar syrup (see page 19)
120 ml/4 fl oz G. H. Mumm Champagne

Place a bay leaf in the base of a champagne flute. Pour the sugar syrup over, then top with champagne.

{ PUNCHES }

SEAFARER'S PUNCH

{ Delicious on its own, this is also a drink that works as a punch
to share. It was created for an Elizabethan-themed drinks
night we hosted aboard the *Golden Hinde* – a replica of Sir
Francis Drake's ship which is moored in dry dock on the South
Bank in London. Arrack is a spirit made from palm sugar.

30 ml/1 fl oz Earl Grey tea
40 ml/1½ fl oz Ceylon Arrack
10 ml/2 tsp Ron Zacapa or Pusser's rum
10 ml/2 tsp port
20 ml/⅔ fl oz sugar syrup (see page 19)
30 ml/1 fl oz lemon juice
Prosecco to taste

Make the Earl Grey tea in advance to a ratio of 5g/1 tsp loose leaf
Earl Grey tea per 100 ml/3½ fl oz water. You can cold-brew this – no
need to mess around with hot water. Even easier still is to use a couple
of tea bags. Pour off the tea before it extracts too much tannin – to
your taste.

Assemble the ingredients in a shaker and shake with a handful of ice
cubes before serving in a wine glass or teacup.

For a party:
Simply extrapolate the ingredients to the number of serves you want,
then add all the ingredients into a punch bowl over a large block of ice,
stir and then pour in a bottle of Prosecco. Ladle into teacups: classic
punch would have been served in teacups at coffee houses across
London in the 17th and 18th centuries.

CAPTAIN'S PUNCH

{ This is a recipe created for the Lost Lagoon, where we built
an enormous subterranean lake in the basement of a shopping
centre in west London in collaboration with Captain Morgan.
This recipe follows the rules of the rhyme (see page 15) and you
can basically adapt it any which way you want. Swap out lime
for lemon, grapefruit or pink grapefruit. Change maple syrup for
honey syrup, grenadine or coconut cream. Switch out rum for
whisky, brandy or vodka. No apricot juice? No problem. Turn to
real tea, fruit tea, fruit soda or coconut water. Just follow the
rule and you shouldn't go far wrong.

10 ml/2 tsp lime juice
20 ml/⅔ fl oz maple syrup
30 ml/1 fl oz Captain Morgan Spiced Rum
40 ml/1½ fl oz apricot juice
Dash of Angostura bitters
Freshly grated nutmeg to garnish

Assemble all the liquid ingredients in a shaker and add a scoop of ice
cubes. Shake it to wake it, then strain into a goblet or wine glass and
garnish with freshly grated nutmeg.

For a party:
Simply extrapolate the ingredients to the number of serves you want,
then add all the ingredients into a punch bowl over a large block of ice
and stir.

COCKTAIL BASICS

Cocktails shouldn't be some mystifying dark art, one that's only practised by professional bartenders. Everyone should be able to make them. All you need to do is master a few techniques and understand the terminology. Follow recipes to the letter, then, as you gain confidence, you'll begin to recognize the ways you can adapt drinks, play with flavours and create your own twists. This is the gist of cocktail bartending.

ICE

Ice is one of the most important ingredients in cocktails. It is not just used for its ability to rapidly chill drinks, it also provides essential dilution in cocktails. This opens up flavours in the spirits and softens the burn of alcohol. Ice, however, comes in many forms, and you can find many online recommendations for making your own – we love www.alcademics.com/ice for its comprehensive approach to the science of ice.

CUBED ICE

You can make this yourself using ice cube trays but if you are making cocktails more than occasionally it's far easier to buy bags of ready-made ice. Make sure you use ice cubes that are a decent size: if the cubes are too small or the shape too complex then you'll end up with too much dilution in the drink. Bigger is better – think of the huge ice cubes you get in Spain – and on trend. If you live in a city, you can easily find ice makers who can deliver good-quality ice in 12kg bags – perfect for parties.

CRUSHED ICE

Essential for juleps, tiki drinks and more. Either buy it, or better still (as shop-bought ice can be too small and melt too easily) make it yourself. Some brands offer canvas coin bags as gifts, which allows you to fill it with cubed ice and set about it with a rolling pin. In lieu of that, wrap cubed ice in a tea towel and bash away. Drain off any excess water before adding the ice to drinks. Again, if you live in a city, you can use professional suppliers.

BLOCK ICE AND ICE TOOLS

This is probably the biggest ice innovation that's occurred since we first published this book in 2011. Block ice is crystal clear, and people seem to love it more than it deserves, despite it merely being frozen water. As well as being perfect for punch as one large 'iceberg', you can also hack directly off this for individual drinks using a raft of newly available tools (try www.cocktailkingdom.com) such as ice tridents, saws and picks. You can buy blocks of ice from specialist suppliers, but you can also try and make your own, which allows you to add your choice of decorative botanicals to the mix. Again, follow online instructions which can advise on the best way to avoid cloudy ice when making it at home. Try: www.alcademics.com/index-of-ice-experiments-on-alcademics

ICE BUCKET AND TONGS

How big a bucket you require depends on what sort of party you are planning, but you'll want to keep your ice somewhere that's insulated and can catch any drips. There are plenty of nice tongs on the market – don't let your guests catch you using your hands!

COCKTAIL TECHNIQUES

SHAKING AND STIRRING

Most cocktails need to be either shaken or stirred with ice, depending on the ingredients and the desired texture that you want from the finished drink.

SHAKING

Some people argue that all cocktails should be shaken, even conventionally stirred ones. It wakes the drink up, or adds life to it, so they say. This is because of the profound difference in mouthfeel that shaking adds, by introducing lots of tiny air bubbles into the drink, as well as it being the preferred method for drinks requiring citrus juice or fruit. Tiny bits of ice will also become incorporated into the drink – some bartenders strain these bits out while others prefer to leave them in the final drink.

BOSTON SHAKER

This has two parts: a mixing glass and a metal shaker; they are used individually for mixing drinks and together to form a shaker.

To master the Boston, always add the ingredients into the mixing glass so that you can get a sense of how much liquid is going in. When all the liquids are in, fill the glass with ice so that it is level with the brim. Bring down the metal part over the glass and tap it firmly with the heel of your hand to form a seal. To check, lift the metal part slightly and it should bring the glass with it. Pick up the shaker with two hands and, holding it with one hand at each end and with the metal part at the bottom, shake rapidly and firmly.

Shake it like you mean it – channel machine gun rapidity (and noise) rather than just wafting it around – for about 15 seconds, then place the shaker metal part down on the worktop.

Holding the shaker in one hand, with two fingers wrapped securely around the metal and two around the glass, hit the rim of the metal part with the heel of your other hand. The seal between the two parts should break but this can be hard to master because the freezing temperatures affect the pressure inside. If it doesn't work first time, turn the shaker slightly and try again.

With a little practice the Boston shaker is quicker to use than the 'cobbler' or three-piece shaker – these are all-metal shakers that have a screw-on lid and built-in strainer and usually recommended for beginners. There's also a rather nice glass Kilner shaker that has its own strainer. But prefer the Boston, the professionals' choice.

Don't use cutesy plastic shakers. You won't be able to feel when you have reached the correct temperature.

STIRRING

Stirring is the right choice for spirit-heavy cocktails like Martinis and Sazeracs, without juices or mixers. This can be done in a glass mixing glass, metal shaker or similar. Adding a good handful (best not to use your hand) of large ice cubes will blend and cool the drink while keeping the cocktail smooth and silky. You'll end up with a clean marriage of flavours and a crystal-clear cocktail.

MIXING GLASS

You can mix a 'stirred' drink in anything, although having a proper mixing glass is surprisingly rewarding. It allows you to get a sense of how much dilution you are creating through stirring. It's important that the glass is tempered, as this means it won't crack when subjected to extreme changes in temperature or if you get violent with the ice cubes. The Japanese-style Yarai mixing glass is hugely popular right now. Again, try www.cocktailkingdom.com

The secret to good stirring is smoothness and elegance. Professional bartenders pride themselves on keeping not just their elbow still, but their wrist too, only moving their fingers the least amount required to turn the stack of ice in the glass, while holding the base of the mixing glass with the fingertips of their other hand, so as not to warm it with their body heat.

Successful stirring, and the ability to know when to stop, comes with practice. Don't be afraid to taste the mix with your bar spoon before you strain, to assess dilution and chill – just be sure to wash it rather than stick it back in.

BUILDING

This refers to assembling a drink in the glass in which it is to be served. Simply measure out the components, add ice, give it a stir and add any garnish.

PRE-BATCHING

Certainly one of the most prevailing techniques that has helped democratize cocktails over the last decade, pre-batching is what's behind seeing cocktails on tap in increasing numbers of bars. It's actually dead easy to master. It works best with non-perishable, high alcohol content drinks – cocktails such as Negronis can last and last (and you can also potentially age the mix in miniature barrels) but you can also use the technique for just about any mixed drink, including with perishable components. Think of it this way: when you make a punch, you're basically pre-batching. Don't pre-batch fizzy components – you can add them later to preserve the bubbles.

To pre-batch any cocktail, simply extrapolate the recipe for one portion by the number of serves you want in a large vessel that will fit in your fridge. Combine all the liquid components, then add 10% of the total liquid volume in water. This integrates the dilution you'd otherwise get from shaking or stirring individual drinks. Refrigerate the mix, then when you're ready to serve, add any fizzy components and simply pour over fresh ice. Easy peasy.

BAR SPOON

This has two functions: measuring (a bar spoon is a commonly requested measure in recipes) and stirring cocktails in a mixing glass, or giving a highball a final whizz before you serve it. At the non-spoon end they can have either weighty balls or flat ends for gently muddling mint for Mojitos, or a thin fork for garnishes.

MUDDLER

This is a mini baseball-bat-shaped pestle designed to crush herbs, fruit and sugar in the bottom of a shaker or sugar in the base of an old-fashioned glass. The best ones are made of wood, although you can get plastic ones. If you don't have one it's not hard to improvise (use a rolling pin).

STRAINERS

However you prepare your drink you will need to remove ice and other ingredients from your shaken or stirred cocktail.

HAWTHORNE STRAINER

This straining device is characterized by a curved spring. It's designed to fit the metal part of a Boston shaker. The sprung end pushes against the inside of the shaker to ensure a snug fit. Try to master picking up the metal part of the shaker and the Hawthorne strainer in one hand.

MESH STRAINER

These are often used in tandem with the Hawthorne and Boston shaker. Holding the mesh strainer in your other hand, pour the liquid from the Boston, it will, of course, pass through the Hawthorne strainer first, and then the mesh strainer, which will catch any remaining ice shards. This creates more 'perfect' drinks in terms of appearance, but many people like the glittery effect of these tiny ice shards and some like the feel on the tongue.

JULEP STRAINER

This one is used more in conjunction with a glass mixing glass once you have stirred a cocktail. As stirring isn't nearly so violent as shaking, the ice won't have broken up to the same extent and you don't need to worry about ice shards in your drink. This mini colander should fit just inside the circumference of your mixing glass.

SPIRIT MEASURE

A spirit measure, or jigger, is important for making consistent drinks. The double-ended type is the most useful: one end measures a double and the other a single. The actual measure will vary: it all depends on how much booze you want to put in your cocktail. A 50 ml/25 ml jigger makes perfect sense.

MEASURING

The measures in our recipes are given in millilitres (with imperial conversions). We feel that this is best, as it allows you to get a sense of the proportions of the ingredients in each cocktail. Each recipe (except where stated) is for one drink. So when you are making more than one cocktail simply remember to multiply the other ingredients accordingly. As you gain in confidence and experience, you may find that you are able to consider the recipes in 'parts' – quantities in proportion to one another. This is an invaluable development in your ability to interpret cocktails, understand the similarities between different drinks, and adapt cocktails to your own specification.

It is acceptable to shake or stir enough mixture to make two or, at a push, three, cocktails. Any more and you are not going to get enough interaction between ice and liquid to get the required dilution or chill. But while professionals can judge how much they are pouring direct from a bottle, we recommend using a jigger to ensure consistency.

CITRUS JUICER/SQUEEZER

You can juice lemons or limes by hand – say with a wooden lemon reamer – but a proper squeezer makes all the difference. The 'elbow' type are the best – just make sure you insert the fruit counterintuitively – it should be flesh down, and sit proud of the mould, only filling it when you squeeze, turning the fruit inside out for maximum juice.

CHOPPING BOARD AND KNIFE

It's worth keeping a separate board just for use in cocktails. Cocktail flavours can be subtle and it's best if they are not attacked by a slice of orange cut on a garlic-infused board. One simple knife should be enough for cutting up fruit, preparing garnishes and peels. A peeler may make the job easier though.

BOTTLE OPENER AND CORKSCREW

For crown-capped mixers, beer and wine.

GLASSWARE

Choosing the right glass for any given cocktail is paramount. The rules tend to have evolved because they work in partnership with the liquid that they contain and the behavioural semiotics of using the glasses – essentially how we naturally interact with the drink, its temperature, the duration of consumption, that sort of thing.

MARTINI/UP-SERVES

For short drinks (this simply means low-volume drinks of up to 100 ml/3½ fl oz) you'll need stemmed cocktail glasses – also known as martini glasses – for serving drinks 'straight up' (without ice). The stems mean the heat of your hand won't warm the drink within. We're not fans of stemless martini glasses that come with separate lower sections that you can pack with crushed ice, to rest the top bit in. For martini-style cocktail glasses it's important that they are not too big: we reckon that glasses that take about 100 ml/3½ fl oz comfortably are spot on. Any bigger and you'll be time travelling back to the 1980s.

And talking of the 1980s, while coupettes and coupes (also known as champagne saucers) have become de rigueur for martini-style serves, we're still keen to throw some classic V-shaped glasses into the mix.

OLD FASHIONED

You'll also need low tumblers, often called 'old-fashioned' glasses, for serving drinks 'on the rocks' (with ice). The chunkier the better here: the weight holds the cold better, and the weight subconsciously channels perceptions of quality about the contents.

HIGHBALLS

For long drinks you need tall, narrow 'highball' glasses: they come in various sizes; large ones are better for drinks served with lots of crushed or cubed ice. You may wish to add straws for service, especially for crushed ice drinks, but we cannot condone single-use plastic straws. Either invest in quality metal ones, or buy paper or bamboo sustainable straws.

FLUTES/WINE GLASSES

Champagne flutes are a must for champagne cocktails and are designed, of course, for drinking champagne by concentrating the CO_2 released from the constantly bursting bubbles in just the right quantity – but not enough to overwhelm. Wine glasses which are usually more narrow at the top are designed for similar reasons – to concentrate aromas – but are still useful for some cocktails. In addition, the stems keep the drink itself away from your body heat.

NICK 'N' NORA

These small-stemmed glasses are perfect for short serves where you're channelling elegance and aren't serving on the rocks. You'll see them everywhere in good cocktail bars and they can serve as alternatives to up-serves classically served in martini glasses or coupes.

OTHER GLASSES

You'll read elsewhere about other types of cocktail glassware – hurricanes, slings, julep tins, margarita glasses, mule cups, tiki mugs, copas and copitas, sours, snifters and schooners, piña colada glasses and more. We're confident you'll get by with our more singular selection above.

That said, we remain partial to hollowed-out fruit – pineapples are perfect here. Did someone say kitsch?

CHILLING GLASSES

Cocktails are best when they are extremely cold. You'll see bartenders chill glasses quickly by adding a scoop of crushed ice into a glass as they prepare a drink in a shaker or mixing glass, and then discarding the crushed ice just before they pour the drink in. This is essential when you think their glasses probably just came out of a hot dishwasher. It's better practice at home to put your glasses in a freezer for 20–30 minutes. Not only will they be super chilled when you remove them but they will become nicely frosted instantly as they react to the ambient temperature.

SEMIOTICS/CROSSMODALISM

Most people already have a selection of tumblers, highballs and champagne flutes at home. However, it's worth searching for decent glassware as it makes cocktails more enjoyable and can improve the taste of the drink. This is all down to the semiotics and the subconscious flavour and quality cues that our brain makes before we taste the drink: their size, weight, colour and level of decorative fanciness all strongly communicate what's inside before you taste it. Drinking cocktails out of jam jars just doesn't taste the same as when sipped from cut crystal. A crudely ridged rim, for example, appears rustic and simple compared to a finely lipped glass.

This is crossmodalism at work: this refers to how all your senses work together. In the case of taste, it's not just your tongue that does the tasting. We've spent a lot of time investigating crossmodalism, not least in our collaborations with the Crossmodal Laboratory at the University of Oxford, and this stuff matters, and we know it to be hugely influential in our perception of taste, flavour, quality and price.

RESOURCES

BUYING ALCOHOL
GERRY'S WINES & SPIRITS
Real experts with an incredibly wide stock.
Worldwide mail order.
74 Old Compton St, London W1D 4UW
www.gerrys.uk.com
UTOBEER
All your obscure beer needs, and on our
doorstep too.
24 Borough Market, London SE1 1TL
www.boroughmarket.org.uk/traders/
utobeer
THE WHISKY EXCHANGE
Not just whisky but an exhaustive
supply of all sorts of spirits, liqueurs
and accompaniments at all price points.
Several London stores as well as
worldwide mail order.
2 Bedford St, London WC2E 9HH
www.whiskyexchange.com

BROWSING ALCOHOL
HEDONISM WINES
The next level in luxury booze hunting,
with beautiful displays that spill out on to
the pavement.
3-7 Davies St, Mayfair, London W1K 3LD
www.hedonism.co.uk
SELFRIDGES
Worth a look whenever we're nearby as
its wine shop is extremely well-stocked.
400 Oxford St, London W1A 1AB
www.selfridges.com

COCKTAIL EQUIPMENT
COCKTAIL KINGDOM
Everything forthe budding bartender as
well as more obscure items.
www.cocktailkingdom.com
CHEEKY TIKI
Inject tropical décor and drinking
paraphernalia into all aspects
of your life. Worldwide shipping.
8B, Queens Yard, White Post Lane,
London E9 5EN
www.cheekytiki.com
JOHN LEWIS
A wide range of glassware from our
favourite suppliers – Riedel, Villeroy &
Boch, LSA International among others –
and swift delivery.
www.johnlewis.com

SOME WEBSITES
ALCADEMICS
Get your geek on and dive deep into
many different topics.
www.alcademics.com
COOKING ISSUES
Specialist drinks development and
experiments from a scientist.
www.cookingissues.com
SAVOY STOMP
A discontinued blog but an amazing
resource into the trials and tribulations
of making cocktails.
www.savoystomp.flannestad.com

INDEX

absinthe: Death in the
        Afternoon 105
    Sazerac 81
armagnac 77
arrack: Seafarer's Punch 111

Baileys Original: Winter
Wonder 51
Batanga 70
Black Velvet Royale 103
Bloody Mary 63
bourbon see whiskey
brandy 76–95
    Brandy Crusta 87
    Brandy Snap 95
    Champagne Cocktail 104
    Espresso Cognac-Tail 90
    Iced Tea Club 87
    Maple Colada 92
    Pisco Sour 83
    Sazerac 81
    Shipwreck Sour 84
    Sidecar 78
    Soyer au Champagne 107
    Yuzu 75 88

Calvados: Shipwreck Sour
        84
Captain's Punch 112
champagne 96–109
    Black Velvet Royale 103
    Champagne Cocktail 104
    Champagne Scotchtail
        47
    Champion Cocktail 109
    Death in the Afternoon
        105
    French 75 100
    Kir Royale 102
    Mexican 55 69
    Rose Fizz 42
    Soyer au Champagne 107
    Yuzu 75 88

champagne bottles: sabrage
        98–9
    sizes 99
Champion Cocktail 109
cider brandy: Shipwreck
        Sour 84
citrus zest garnishes 18
Clover Club 34
Coca-Cola: Batanga 70
coffee: Corrected Espresso
        Martini 62
    Espresso Cognac-Tail 90
cognac see brandy
Corrected Espresso
        Martini 62
crème de cassis: Black
        Velvet Royale 103
    Kir Royale 102

Daiquiri 57
Dark 'n' Stormy Monk 56
Death in the Afternoon 105
Drambuie: Brandy Snap 95
Dry Martini 30

East Meets North 44
equipment 118–20
espresso: Corrected
        Espresso Martini 62
    Espresso Cognac-Tail 90

flips/blended/warm
        cocktails: Brandy Snap
        95
    Maple Colada 92
    Winter Wonder 51
Formula E 64
French 75 100

G&T 22
garnishes 18–19
Gimlet 25
gin 20–35
    Clover Club 34
    French 75 100
    G&T 22

Gimlet 25
Hanky Panky 24
Negroni 27
Orbium Martinez 32
Peach Gin Fizz 30
Pink Gin 24
Sting & Tonic 22
Strawberry & Cream
        Ramos Gin Fizz 33
White Cargo 29
ginger beer: Dark 'n'
        Stormy Monk 56
glassware 121–4
Green Tea & Grain 48
Guinness: Black Velvet
        Royale 103

Hanky Panky 24
highballs 16–17, 121
    Batanga 70
    Bloody Mary 63
    Green Tea & Grain 48
    Iced Tea Club 87
    Mojito 54
    Nuclear Piña Colada 58
    Paloma 73
    Sting & Tonic 22
    Yuzu 75 88

ice 114–15
ice cream: Soyer au
        Champagne 107
    White Cargo 29
Iced Tea Club 87
Irish whiskey 37

jasmine tea: East Meets
        North 44
Julep, Mint 39

Kahlua: Corrected
        Espresso Martini 62
Kir Royale 102

lime juice: Captain's Punch
        112

Gimlet 25
Margarita 74
Mojito 54
Manhattan 38
Maple Colada 92
Margarita 74
Martini 14–15, 17, 121
    Corrected Espresso
        Martini 62
    Dry Martini 30
    Espresso Cognac-Tail 90
    Formula E 64
    Gimlet 25
    Hanky Panky 24
    Manhattan 38
    Mint Julep 39
    Orbium Martinez 32
    Pink Gin 24
Mexican 55 69
mezcal 68
    Mezcal Old Fashioned
        68
    Mr Twit's Dirty Negroni
        28
Mint Julep 39
Mr Twit's Dirty Negroni 28
Mojito 54

Negroni 27
    Mr Twit's Dirty Negroni
        28
nettle cordial: Sting & Tonic
    22
Nuclear Piña Colada 58

Old Fashioned 15, 17, 40, 121
    Dark 'n' Stormy Monk 56
    Mezcal Old Fashioned 68
    Mr Twit's Dirty Negroni
        28
    Negroni 27
    Sazerac 81
Orbium Martinez 32

Paloma 73
Peach Gin Fizz 30

Piña Colada, Nuclear 58
pineapple: Nuclear Piña
    Colada 58
Pink Gin 24
Pisco Sour 83
punches 15–17, 110–13
    Captain's Punch 112
    East Meets North 44
    Seafarer's Punch 111
    White Cargo 29

Rose Fizz 42
rum 52–9
    Captain's Punch 112
    Daiquiri 57
    Dark 'n' Stormy Monk 56
    Mojito 54
    Nuclear Piña Colada 58
    Rum Daisy 57
    Seafarer's Punch 111
rye whiskey see whiskey

sabrage, champagne bottles
    98–9
Sazerac 81
Seafarer's Punch 111
Shipwreck Sour 84
Sidecar 78
soda water: Paloma 73
sourness 19
sours 13, 17
    Brandy Crusta 87
    Clover Club 34
    Daiquiri 57
    Margarita 74
    Peach Gin Fizz 30
    Pisco Sour 83
    Rum Daisy 57
    Shipwreck Sour 84
    Sidecar 78
    Strawberry & Cream
        Ramos Gin Fizz 33
    Whiskey Sour 39
Soyer, Alexis 106–7
Soyer au Champagne 107
Sting & Tonic 22

Strawberry & Cream
    Ramos Gin Fizz 33
sugar syrup 19
sweetness 19

techniques 116–20
tequila 66–75
    Batanga 70
    Margarita 74
    Mexican 55 69
    Mezcal Old Fashioned 68
    Paloma 73
tomato juice: Bloody Mary
    63
tonic water: Sting & Tonic 22

vermouth: Dry Martini 30
    Hanky Panky 24
    Mr Twit's Dirty Negroni 28
    Negroni 27
vodka 60–5
    Bloody Mary 63
    Corrected Espresso
        Martini 62
    Formula E 64

whiskey 37
    Manhattan 38
    Mint Julep 39
    Old Fashioned 40
    Whiskey Sour 39
    Winter Wonder 51
whisky 36–51
    Champagne Scotchtail 47
    East Meets North 44
    Green Tea & Grain 48
    Rose Fizz 42
White Cargo 29
Winter Wonder 51

Yuzu 75 88

FURTHER READING

Amis, Kingsley *Everyday Drinking: The Distilled Kingsley Amis*; Baker Jr, Charles H. *Jigger, Beaker & Glass – Drinking Around the World*; Berry, Jeff *Beachbum Berry's Potions of the Caribbean*; Brown, Jared and Miller, Anistatia *Spirituous Journey, A History of Drink (Book One: From the Birth of Spirits to the Birth of the Cocktail)*; *Spirituous Journey, A History of Drink (Book Two: From Publicans to Master Mixologists)*; Chetiyawardana, Ryan *Good Things to Drink with Mr Lyan and Friends*; Craddock, Harry *The Savoy Cocktail Book*; Curtis, Wayne *And a Bottle of Rum: A History of the New World in Ten Cocktails*; DeGroff, Dale *The Craft of the Cocktail*; De Voto, Bernard *The Hour: A Cocktail Manifesto*; Embury, David A. *The Fine Art of Mixing Drinks*; Grogan, Peter *Grogan's Companion to Drink: the A to Z of Alcohol*; Kaye, Jordan and Altier, Marshall *How to Booze: Exquisite Cocktails and Unsound Advice*; Kosmas, Jason and Zaric, Dushan. *Speakeasy*; McGovern, Patrick E. *Uncorking the Past: the Quest for Wine, Beer and other Alcoholic Beverages*; Meehan, Jim. *The PDT Cocktail Book*; O'Neil, Darcy *Fix the Pumps*; Robinson, Jancis *Jancis Robinson on the Demon Drink*; Rowley, Matthew B. *Moonshine!*; Schmidt, William *The Flowing Bowl: What and When to Drink*; Schnakenberg, Robert *Old Man Drinks: Recipes, Advice, and Barstool Wisdom*; Stephenson, Tristan *The Curious Bartender – The Artistry and Alchemy of Creating the Perfect Cocktail*; Warner, Jessica *Craze: Gin and Debauchery in an Age of Reason*; Watman, Max *Chasing the White Dog: An Amateur Outlaw's Adventures in Moonshine*; Wondrich, David *Punch: The Delights (and Dangers) of the Flowing Bowl*; *Imbibe!*

ROLL OF HONOUR

A huge thanks to the extended Bompas & Parr creative and production team which brings our events and commercial activations to life. Harry and I really couldn't do it without you. In addition, we would like to single out a few people. Ian Cameron, our creative brand director who has led most of our consultancy projects for drinks brands over the past five years, collaborating with a roll-call of international bartenders, has extensively updated and rewritten this edition – and even made the drinks for the photoshoot. Adam Lock, our bar development manager for several years, was behind many of the weird and wonderful cocktail recipes and signature twists on classics. Dan Price, our art editor, took many of the photos (unless separately attributed below).

We also want to thank our editors at Pavilion Books, in particular Fiona Holman and Stephanie Milner.

PHOTO CREDITS

Bompas & Parr Pages 23 26 31 35 41 45 50 55 59 71 72 75 82 85 101 112 122
Rob Lawson Pages 1 43 49 79 80
Charlie Surbey Front and back cover Pages 7 65 86 89 91 93 94 108